Unfaithful Hearts

Camille Babin

Copyright © 2019 Camille Babin

All rights reserved.

ISBN-13: 978-1-7320903-3-0

DEDICATION

I want to give praise and honor to
the Almighty King, Jesus Christ, my Lord and Savior.
Thank you for giving me the strength and the audacity to
release the words you've placed in my heart.

To the love of my life, my husband,
Jean-Claude.
Thank you for being committed to loving me each and
every day. I love you.

Contents

INTRODUCTION 1

PART I: DEFINING ONENESS

1 And the Two shall become One 5
2 Love & Respect 14
3 Naked and Unashamed 26

PART II: CHASING ONENESS

4 Dating with broken bones 38
5 Too low, too high 49
6 No strings attached 62

PART III: DEFILING ONENESS

7 What about Love? 70
8 Sex traps 79
9 Out of order 92

PART II: RESTORING ONENESS

10 Facing the past 105
11 Renewing your mind 112
12 Returning to Him 121

ACKNOWLEDGMENTS

"For the word of God is alive and active. Sharper than any double-edged sword, it penetrates even to dividing soul and spirit, joints and marrow; it judges the thoughts and attitudes of the heart." Hebrews 4:12

I would like to thank all the men and women who have wept and continue to weep on behalf of God's children, for their salvation and transformation in Jesus name.

The soldiers in the kingdom of God who never cease to put up a fight, showing love and mercy while standing on the truth of the Word.

All the people in my life who have not yet accepted Jesus as their Lord and Savior.
May they hear your plea and come back to you.

To those who hunger and thirst after the Lord
May you find him amid the confusion and the chaos around.

INTRODUCTION

Last summer, I went on a mission trip to my hometown, Abidjan in Cote d'Ivoire. I was very reluctant to go since I was unsure about my ability to handle the various things the Lord had revealed to me. Then one day, He said, "I will never send you anywhere else if you can't face the giant in your own country.... How would you tell people to fight, when you wouldn't do so yourself?" Yes, I admit, it would have been very hypocritical. In my mind, I thought if God is sending me there, it's because He wants me to experience some of the things I was getting ready to write in my next book *Fight*. However, it didn't take me long to realize that His plan was not quite what I anticipated...as usual.

On the way back from Cote d'Ivoire, I was at the Liberty airport in Newark, waiting for my flight home. It certainly was the shortest, and most interesting layover I spent in my entire life. While I was waiting, I heard the Lord's voice whispering very distinctively to me in French "Cœurs infidèles" or "Unfaithful hearts." I could not figure out what this meant, but I knew it was worth recording. I grabbed a piece of paper and scribbled every word that kept coming. At first, I thought there were ideas for a blog post until I was given sections and chapters. It became clear at that point that this was the title of a book. It didn't take a second for me to say "Ok, Lord," thinking it will not be anytime soon or at least after I was done writing *Fight*, remember the mission trip? Well, a couple of months later, I was still not released to write *Fight*, though I kept receiving prophetic words from various people, friends, and family telling me "the Lord wants you to write, He wants you to work on the book." I began to feel a bit confused; I had no idea in which direction He was taking me. What book is this about, Lord? No answer. And I still couldn't write a thing.

About three days ago, during our intercession prayer, the Lord took me to a high place. I could see snakes on the ground, floating around the people in churches, and as we were praying and pleading the blood of Jesus, all the snakes started to die, drowned in the huge pool of blood. Then the Lord spoke about His wrath, His upcoming judgment. I saw his hand rising as if He was ready to let it come down on his people. There was no emotion; I felt chills, it was very dry, cold and stern, then I saw a bright, almost blinding light. For a second, I prayed for Him to take me away into the light, and suddenly, I started to weep, uncontrollably. I felt like my heart was being ripped apart. I began to beg and plead for the Lord to extend His grace and mercy upon all of us. I prayed that He would draw His people back to Him, that He will give us hearts of flesh, hearts that will repent and turn away from our sinful nature.

So, today, I have the answer, and I'll wait no further. But why am I telling you all of this? I don't know. One thing I know: I must share what He puts in my heart. He wants to keep us informed about what is happening and help us understand the times we currently live in. He will use anyone to make sure His words touch as many people as possible. Many of us have wept, cried out to Him, in the secret places of our homes and our hearts – this book may come as an answer to some of our prayers. The answers may not be what we want to hear, and they may not even be what we are willing or able to accept or recognize, but who can keep God silent when He has decided to speak?

I can tell you right from the start, the objective of this book is not to bring guilt, shame or condemnation to anyone. Since I am the one to relay these words, I believe I am also the first recipient, the first one to receive correction, rebuke or discipline. He is talking to me as much as He is talking to you, and we know that God's truth brings life to our souls.

It is time to walk in the freedom that Christ has set before us. We must, therefore, rip the bandage off, and let Jehovah Rapha, our Healer, bind up our wounds. Let us invite His Holy Spirit to guide us and hold our hands while we embark on this journey of truth, healing, and restoration.

I pray that His word will bring such conviction to all of us that we will no longer walk in the bondage of sin. I also pray that we allow Him to take us back to the various places He wants us to revisit to close the doors no man will ever be able to reopen – doors of oppression, confusion, and sin.

PART 1

DEFINING "ONENESS"

1
...AND THE TWO SHALL BECOME ONE

In the beginning, God created mankind in his image; He created them male and female, [1] both, from the same source, breathed life into them and commanded them to be fruitful and multiply, subdue the earth and rule over, together, as one.
From that time, God's spirit was inhabiting the hearts of men, constantly guiding, leading, and drawing them into his presence, keeping them close, until the fall. Adam and Eve allowed another spirit to penetrate their hearts and affect their minds. They gave way to the serpent to dwell in their midst, producing doubt, mistrust, shame, guilt, blame, and rejection. The light that was created to shine bright was suddenly crowned with a shade. There was no longer one voice, but two; two distinct people instead of one. God's masterpiece was instantly tainted with sin, making it impossible for all of us to remain in the sacred place with the Master.
Unity was not just between Adam and Eve, it was a triangular affair with our Lord. And as long as men submitted to the Father, there was total cohesion between them, a symbiosis so perfect that they could live in complete trust and transparency, as one man, exactly like the Father anticipated. Why should we be concerned about what had happened before the fall

---

[1] Gen. 1:27

since Jesus came to stand in the gap for all of us, to reclaim the oneness?
Yes, Jesus succeeded where men failed. He broke the curse of sin and gave us victory. Where men could not resist temptation, Jesus resisted the devil and made him flee. That should captivate our attention – the way a husband and wife lived before they were evicted from the garden, that time when they knew the heart and the will of God and gave Him their undivided attention. Yes, that time is very crucial as it's our ultimate blueprint. It gives us the perfect insight on God's intent for marriage, a profound glimpse into His heart. If we could, for a second, understand and visualize how things were in the beginning, it might prevent us from repeating the same mistakes. God created us in His image; it's not about what we look like on the outside. For God is not concerned about the outward appearance[2]; He looks at our hearts. And our heart reflects the spirit we carry. Whose spirit are you carrying? Why do you think Jesus said that we are defiled not by what goes into our mouths, but what comes out of it?[3] Once again, it's all about the hearts. The spirit God breathed into the nostrils of men,[4] must go out through our words and actions, as evidence of the spirit that lives inside of us. Do you remember the adage: "Show me your friends and I'll show you who you are"? Well, with Jesus it will certainly sound something like this: "show me your heart and I'll tell you whose spirit you carry."
The fact that men sinned and fell short of the glory of God by no means disqualifies us for the race. Jesus came to this world in a human body to give us an opportunity to start over. We get another chance to

---

2 1 Sam.16:7
3 Matthew 15:11
4 Gen. 2:7

know Him, hear His voice and access every treasure He had in store for us before we were even formed. He wants to reveal His will and is waiting for us to do our part: work to bring him delight, but what kind of work are we referring to? The work of our hearts: our Worship. It's worship that brings us back into the presence of the Father. Do I hear someone asking: "what about prayer? Isn't prayer the key to unlock God's promises? Or if it's worship, why did Jesus ask us to pray without ceasing?"

True, sincere prayer will always lead to worship. Not the self- centered prayer, not the "Lord give me this" or "give me that." Prayer that solely focuses on "self" will never take you into the presence of God. Remember, prayer is our communication with our maker, a time of communion, exchange, and intimacy. There is no intimacy without reciprocity. When God gave us access to the Holy of Holies, He didn't ask for anything in return, except for our hearts. He wants our hearts back, the same way it was in the beginning.

Prayer and worship are inextricably connected. Prayer is what God gives us. It's His word, His Spirit; it is the secret He so kindly shared with us to give us entrance to his courts. Prayer removes the scales from our eyes and helps us see God in all His splendor and majesty. Our worship is like a stethoscope, allowing us to hear God's heartbeat – discerning His will concerning His people as we begin to experience a new dimension of His presence. We get a glimpse of the magnitude of His love for us.

We are the bride of Christ; He is our bridegroom, our husband. What did He command the wife? Submission. He told us, wives, to submit ourselves to our husband. In other words, He could have just said: *worship* your husband, meaning offering our hearts completely, without reservation, withholding nothing, pouring ourselves out like the woman with the alabaster box. Can you paint this picture? What husband could resist the amazing sight of his bride pouring out her love to him? Bathing his feet in the sweet fragrance of her adoration?

Unfortunately, submission no longer implies adoration, devotion or affection; it has become a synonym for degradation and humiliation. As our bridegroom, Jesus never asked us something he wasn't willing to give himself. He loved us first and offered his life for us. Worship is what we ought to give Him: our heart. When Jesus spoke to the Pharisees and the teachers of the law, he highlighted their lack of sincerity. *"You hypocrites! Isaiah was right when he prophesied about you: "These people honor me with their lips, but their hearts are far from me [5]."* They did *almost* everything that the law stated, but their hearts were not in it. They wanted the covenant but refused the relationship, the blessings without the sacrifice.

How many of us today try to get the milk without buying the cow? We want the promises but refuse the One who makes the promises. Can our God, who is Love be content in a loveless relationship? Unless we give our hearts, there is no marriage, no relationship, no intimacy, no communion, therefore no unity. And God's design for marriage is to create a perfect unity through Him. He wants us to be so filled with his spirit that the world will see Him through us. There must be no separation. When we are One, His will become ours, and our lives become a testament of His love and glorious presence.

The time has come and is now for the true worshippers to step forward. *He* is looking for men and women who are not afraid to publicly testify of their love for Him. He

---

[5] Matt. 15:7-9

is looking for those who will no longer hold back, look around, ride the fence or play both sides. He is seeking the ones who will be fully devoted to Him, the ones who will listen to no one but Him and will not be afraid to speak the words revealed by the Holy Spirit. *"My sheep listen to my voice"*[6]. I hear the Lord say: *"Do not be afraid to speak the word I speak through you. Those who know me will know that it is I who speak. And this is how you will recognize those who are called by my name... those who refuse to hear do not want to turn their hearts away from evil, they have already made their choice."*

Why is the Father seeking worshippers that worship in spirit and in truth? First, because He made us in His image, by His spirit. We cannot claim to be of God unless we carry His spirit[7], alive and well within us. If our hearts do not belong to the Father, how can our words testify about Him? It's only when we yield to the Holy Spirit that we can *walk in the Spirit*. He takes total control over our hearts, our minds and our bodies – then, the words we speak will bring life. For God's Word is life; it is the truth that sets us free. His Word sets us free from the bondage of sin, free from the guilt and the shame of our transgressions. Nobody can be filled with the Spirit of the Lord and not walk in truth, for *"the Spirit is truth."* [8] Contrary to what we witness today, there are not multiple truths, but One truth, just like there are not multiple gods, but the one true Living God, Jesus Christ, who died and rose again for the salvation of mankind. Today, the Lord is inviting us all to reassess our positions, our beliefs, and the lies we've allowed to enter our hearts. If you've never done a detox, it's never too late to start. Allow the blood of

---

[6] John 10:27
[7] Romans 8:14
[8] 1 John 5:6

Jesus to wash away every wrong belief, every lie, and every misconception from your system. Allow the Holy Spirit to restore the word of life, word of truth that the enemy is earnestly seeking to twist and bury with his lies.

There can be no compromise with the truth. There is no half-truth. We either walk in light or darkness. We either believe in Jesus, or we don't. We are either male or female, not both. Let's go back to Adam and Eve. The minute they let the serpent in, God had to start all over. His Spirit could no longer dwell in what had been defiled. There was no place for Him in the heart of men. If darkness penetrates, light is compromised, and we know it too well – there can be no unity between light and darkness. For God will never take half of anything. He either has it all or nothing.

For a very long time, most of us have assumed that we could give a little bit here, a little bit there and it will work out fine. We thought we could commit to one thing, but not to the other. I can go to the club on Saturday night and go to church on Sunday morning, read my Bible and watch pornography... Is this what's on the Lord's heart? If we're one with him, then he will give us the desires of our heart. This simply means the Lord will give us the instructions, He will guide us and teach us about what our heart should desire. He will allow us to share the same vision, seek the same goals as *He*. Unfortunately, we have successfully made this about ourselves and what serves *our* purpose.

Our Father yearns to have us all for Himself again, not out of selfish motives; for there is no selfishness in Him, who created us. His desire is to have a close relationship with us, revealing to us the secret plans He has for us. He wants us to become one again, His Spirit dwelling in the secret place of our hearts. Can you hear him calling his bride back into his arms? One mind.

One accord. One purpose.

Today, marriage looks nothing like what God intended. The oneness has vanished though we desperately try to piece it together. The problem is not that marriage is not what God desires, anymore; it simply is that we cannot apply worldly wisdom to God's principles. We cannot achieve unity between two people unless there is unity with the Spirit. You may not have a bad wife or a bad husband as you think, you may just need to redefine and reestablish the foundation of your marriage. Look around! Who are you in this relationship with? Whose spirit are you carrying? You cannot desire God's blessings yet refuse his presence. We just cannot have the promise without the presence for it is the presence that carries the blessings. It is the glory that carries the grace. Marriage is first and foremost a matter of the Spirit, and most marriages fail because we refuse to not only walk in the spirit but work with the Holy Spirit who designed everything. We ought to have a teachable spirit and be willing to learn how to use the tools and weapons He's given us. Imagine this. You're a teacher in a school. Right after you give your students the class syllabus, they pack their bags and walk out. Some may flip through the resources listed on it, read a few articles or so, but they never attend your class, never take any notes, no homework, no quiz, no test, nothing. Should they expect to pass the class? Without question, the answer will be a resounding No. Why do we not expect them to succeed without the teacher's notes or any other kind of assistance, yet expect marriages to thrive without the one who has all the answers, the knowledge, and the power? – the ultimate architect of our lives. I know, times are changing. We are the YouTube/do-it-yourself generation, "self-help" and "self-made." We need nothing from anybody; we wait for nobody to do anything. Do what pleases you. Do what makes you happy. Do "You". Many claim to do it all, have it all or know it all. Is it not God who is Omniscient, Omnipotent and Omnipresent or have we made ourselves more important or as powerful as the Lord? Then we wonder why this generation says they don't need God.

When Heavens and Earth were created, they were given specific territories. The sun and the moon, the plants and the animals, each had a specific function. Men and women were created as one to live as one for eternity. When the full expression of womanhood was not in display, God made a way for her to come out of the men's rib providing him with the companionship, the assistance, the vulnerability and the accountability he needed to fulfill his God-given duties. They were both made to perform the same tasks in a very unique way. The woman was not created to be like man, and vice versa. It was neither by accident, nor by preference that their characteristics were quite different, yet complementary. Both were called to subdue and rule over the earth, bear fruits and multiply, love God and submit. They were both called to love others and make disciples, but we've reduced the purpose of our existence to "self," it is now becoming a power struggle between man and woman. We will come back to this in a later chapter. For now, I want us to go back to the beautiful plan God had in mind when he made women different than men. Our differences were never meant to invalidate his intent for unity. In fact, they were designed to bring and keep us together. Marriage is the absolute representation of the Trinity. God the Father, God the Son and God the Holy Spirit, working in different ways, yet achieving the same purpose of bringing glory to the Father. Men and women were no different. While they are not identical, the result is the same: to bring glory to the Father, together. In our differences, the name of the Father was to be magnified – another remarkable way God displays the fullness of His love. He is a God of balance and order. In both male and female, we see a God who is strong yet soft, powerful yet compassionate, gentle yet impressive... our God is multi-dimensional; His decision to give man a helpmate was to provide us with an opportunity to know Him better, get an understanding of who He is. The same God who heals sent plagues to his disobedient children, the provider who left children in drought and famine. He is the Father who kicked man out of the garden but sent His son to save and His Holy Spirit to watch over us. This is our God. He never contradicts Himself, never work against Himself. Why then, should we try to separate what God has put together?

2
LOVE & RESPECT

Marriage is one of the most important covenants that exists between God and man. He delivered us from the curse of the law, set us free and restored us to a place of victory. Out of His unfailing love, our Father did not waver at the chance to take on human flesh and carry the weight of sin, so that we could reclaim our place in His Kingdom.

When Jesus tells us *He* is the vine, and we are the branches, these are not merely words; they carry a profound meaning that *he* will do whatever it takes to keep us close. As the bridegroom, he bears the responsibility to love, protect, and provide for his bride. What can we learn from our Savior?

Marriage is a decision to enter a relationship not just with another being, but also inviting the Spirit of the Lord to bind and guide us, according to *His* purpose. There is a spiritual dimension of marriage that many are oblivious to, or often disregard. They would consider marriage with a "you and I" mentality, as a contract type relationship rather than a sacred alliance, a God established covenant. And because we've reduced the notion of marriage to a contract, we often approach it from a legal perspective, with respect to our contractual obligations. We become more obsessed about the terms of the offer, who gets the best piece of the pie – we even lay out the dissolution clauses before we enter the agreement. We say yes, but keep one foot out of the door, just in case a better opportunity arises. It never was a question of pleasing God, obeying and following Him, submitting to His will; it was all about seeing our immediate needs fulfilled, satisfying our selfish desires. Marriage appears more as a business transaction, or an auction event, in some cases. If you like it, then put a ring on it...until you don't like it anymore, then you toss the ring out. People are treated with no more value than furniture pieces or articles of clothing, except that the return policy is indefinite; you can return your spouse 30 days, 5 months or 10 years later, without the receipt.

Love is as short as Spring. People fall in and out of love, get married as fast as their eyes can blink, and get divorced even quicker. But this is how the world goes. Life happens. People change, right? We grow apart, have irreconcilable differences; forgetting or choosing to overlook the fact that these same differences were the exact reason why we were so madly in love. How can we be oblivious to the fact that men and women have always been and will always be different? And these differences are the expression of God's sovereignty and power. Only He can create a beautiful synergy between total opposites. He is the only one that can unify our differences, create and maintain the bridge between man and woman, providing understanding, clarity, and even a sense of security and safety that we all long for. He is the only constant in our ever-changing lives. Speaking of differences, let us remember that we could not be more opposite to Christ. Our sinful nature is everything God is not yet *he* chose to love us unconditionally, selflessly giving his life for us. Can anyone of us pretend to be worthy of his love? Do we have any similarity with the Holy One? How can he then call us his bride despite our blemishes and imperfections? What did Jesus see in us? What does he love about us? Let us unpack one of the greatest truths of marriage. Our Father loves absolutely nothing about you or me. For we are selfish, proud, arrogant, liars, unfaithful, irresolute in all our ways. But He loves us, not because of what *we* do, how *we* look or what *we* say, simply because *we are His*. Yes, our God loves us because we were created by *His* Spirit. He chooses to overlook our flaws, weaknesses or shortcomings and offers us His love that is patient, kind, trusting enough to hope for our hearts to totally surrender to His power.

When Adam saw Eve for the first time, he made no remarks about her look or her skills; he saw her with the eyes of the heart, accepted her as his wife, as he recognized the spirit living inside of her. Whose spirit are you carrying? Can someone look at you and recognize Christ? Eve was an intrinsic part of Adam. She was his; the same way we belong to Christ.

Jesus Christ takes us, just as we are and pours out his love for us; love so deep that it makes us want to *be like him*. The love of God always protects, always trusts, always hopes, always perseveres. His love never fails[9]. His love is patient, kind, selfless, forgiving, encouraging. Is this the same kind of love he expects us to have for our spouse? Yes, without a doubt. The only caveat: men have tried for way too long to do the same, relying on their own strength, their own capabilities. And it can't work. It just won't work. We are simply not able to give that kind of love *unless* the Holy Spirit takes over. Hence, the need to have an intimate relationship with God, placing Him on the throne of our hearts.

Love without God is fleeting, and can never outweigh the challenges, the trials we face every day in our lives, our marriages, in the workplace, etc. Our love is impatient, selfish, distrustful. And love that is variable –

---

[9] 1 Corinthians 13:4-7

limited and conditional will never be able to sustain the winds and the storms, the disappointment or the failures.

God created man and marriage. Marriage – that's what He called the relationship He wants to have with us. The bridegroom and his bride, Christ and the church, man and woman, He made them reflect that relationship on a more intimate level.

Without God, there is no marriage. Today, more than ever, we witness the desacralization of the institution of marriage, the perversion and the corruption of our world. We've moved from a covenant relationship to a contract-oriented mentality, forsaking the notion of commitment and sacrifice; they are now "drive-thru" relationships with the exit sign posted right at the entrance. This is the marriage that the world wants because it requires very little or no effort from either party. We stay together, as long as we both can benefit from it – perfect agreement. You get to trade the old for the new, wasting no time to fix it. They say, "why change the light bulb if you can buy a new lamp?". And believers are unashamedly copying the same behavior because we're losing sight of the spiritual dimension of marriage. God has moved from being a must, a requirement to become an optional feature, an accessory. The concept of the Trinity is too hard to understand, too spiritual or just not applicable.

Do we realize that we approach marriage as a passenger traveling on a plane, who, as soon as the plane takes off, throws the pilot out? You may find my illustration extreme, but in many cases, that's' exactly what we do. We pray for a spouse, and as soon as things seem to be moving along our plan, we remit God a pink slip, as if He was our employee.

Let me clarify. God is not interested in a physical threesome, - He is a spiritual being first and foremost-but He must have his place in our individual lives, as well as our marital affairs. He is the one to give the orders, and we obey; not like a tyrant, but with the perfect love that only *He* can give. Jesus calls us into a balanced relationship. Let me explain further. The relationship is by no means balanced due to our equal nature, equal strength or abilities, it is balanced when it is reciprocal. We can never measure up to the love of our God, but he never asked us more than what He poured into us. There is no expectation that we will ever match His *performance* – for lack of a better term; God requires that we give him our heart, not half, not a quarter, the fullness of it; He requires that we trust Him completely with our innermost being.

Read again. "Love always trusts." Love is not abusive, nor deceptive; it does not enslave nor dominate. Love does not control, nor possess. It is a selfless decision to surrender everything that could potentially harm or affect the wellbeing of someone other than yourself. When a parent decides to stop smoking or drinking because of their child's health, we say that is love. If someone gives an organ to a stranger, we recognize love again. Love is a constant decision we make to lay out our heart at the feet of Jesus and trust that he will nurture, protect, and provide everything it needs. We not only trust to receive, but we trust the investment Jesus makes on our behalf. In other words, to love is to trust. Why do we trust God? We trust God because He showed Himself to be trustworthy, right?

Today, I am asking that we revisit all aspects of our life and ask the Holy Spirit to shine His light to bring us into a place of sanctification and holiness. God is truth. In Him there is no ounce of darkness, no existence of lies. When we place Him on the forefront, we can rest assured that He will lead and keep us on the path of light, life, and truth. How often have you read or heard this phrase "Trust God with the choice of your spouse"? It may not always be literal, but there is great truth in this statement. Indeed, God will never come down to bring your spouse as he did with Adam and Eve, He may never tell you "yes this is the man or the woman I have for you", but this statement is only intended to remind you that as long as you live your life seeking to please God, following His directions, submitting to His will rather than presenting your own agenda and begging Him to bless it, you will learn how to recognize His Holy Spirit in your spouse. The Holy Spirit within you will prompt you into discerning the flesh of your flesh, bone of your bones. Love is patient, and we must be patient and know how to wait on the Lord. Too often, we rush into relationships; we get overwhelmed by our emotions and feelings, we go ahead of our Father and blame him when things do not work out. I always refer to Adam and Eve, because they exemplify God's intent for marriage. Adam never pressured God to give him a wife, in fact, he never asked God for a wife, he didn't even know he needed a wife. God saw that Adam was alone and God decided to give him a companion, a helpmate. The beauty in this is God didn't tell Adam what he was going to do; but, because of the relationship they had with each other – love and trust, the Father knew Adam would trust His judgment, His decision. Sure enough, when Adam awoke from his sleep and saw Eve, he said the words we all desire to hear, at least once, "you are mine," "I love you." I am pretty sure if God was not in their midst, Adam's reaction would have been the complete opposite. It most likely would have sounded something like this "who are you?", "what are you doing here?". Since Love was present in the person of our Eternal Father, Adam was able to trust Eve whom he had never met before. That takes us back to the irreconcilable differences once again.

God made no mistakes when He created us male and female and as opposite as we are, He didn't make us this way to leave us trying to figure out how to come together. His plan was never to make us different to separate us, but we have forgotten that He is the link that makes both ends meet, the rope that ties us together, despite our differences. May I be completely accurate, our differences are only in our flesh and soul. "When *God created mankind, He made them in His likeness. He created them male and female and blessed them*[10]." In the spirit, there is no distinction. For the Spirit is One. That's why the Apostle Paul said in Galatians 3: 26-28 *"For you are all children of God through faith in Christ Jesus. And all who have been united with Christ in baptism have put on Christ, like putting on new clothes. There is no longer Jew or Gentile, slave or free, male and female. For you are all one in Christ Jesus."*

Adam did not love Eve in the flesh; he probably didn't even understand his emotions yet. He was fully operating in the Spirit. Therefore, there was no separation between them, for the Spirit of the Father inhabited them both – their connection was spiritual. I said earlier that God was not interested in a physical threesome. God is spirit, and He only meets with us when we choose to walk in the spirit. If we decide to follow our human nature, chase after the desires of the flesh, we will be deceived, and our differences could not become more apparent. The enemy wants us to walk constantly in the flesh. This is the only time he can deceive us. He wants to draw us away from the presence of Christ and make us focus on the things of this world. We must not forget that we are not of this

---

[10] Genesis 5 1-2

world, Jesus paid the price to reclaim our position in the eternal kingdom of the Father. Satan is not after your possessions, he is after your position; he will do everything he can to turn your attention away from the things of the Lord.

In the previous chapter, I highlighted the importance for us to worship the Lord in spirit and truth. Love is the fruit of the Spirit; you can only give love when you are full of the Holy Spirit. You can only feel love when you are full of the Holy Spirit. Love is a person, not an emotion and because we can feel the presence of God, we confuse the person for a feeling. Anytime we say: 'I don't love him/her anymore", or "we fell out of love," you are simply stating that the Holy Spirit is no longer present in your marriage. It may then make perfect sense to wish to end the relationship because there is no marriage without the Spirit of the Lord. When I say, "marriage is spiritual," I am not trying to be religious. If that was not the case, do you believe Jesus would have called us his bride? We must walk in the spirit to experience the grace of marriage and the fullness of God's love. Look at what's happening in the world today, so much hatred, dissension, and division; our differences are magnified only to create enmity. We are unable to love our neighbors because we walk in the flesh. The same is true for our spouse. We constantly seem to highlight their weaknesses and pinpoint everything they do wrong. We no longer work as a team, instead, we've become adversaries.

Our Heavenly Father wants you and I to return to the beginning, where we will once again dwell in his presence, where his love could sustain us, reconcile and harmonize our differences. Let us lead in the spirit of the living God, the one whose love overcomes evil. Once we learn how to operate in the spiritual realm, giving room to the fruit of the Spirit to manifest and overflow, we will witness more people experiencing the grace of having a relationship with Christ.

The key to a successful marriage is solely dependent upon the state of your relationship with Christ. Everything Jesus asked of us, his bride, is love and respect. Many people have a hard time staying committed to the Lord. We seek his hand more often than we seek his face. It's easy to worship and praise him when he makes things happen. If our love for God – who is Holy and perfect is conditional, based upon our emotions of the day or the rewards we can get, how much worse do you think our relationship with our spouse would be?

Today is your chance to take a look at your relationship with the Lord. Is it what it's supposed to be? Does Jesus sit on the front row of your life or is he just a postscript? You already know about the Godhead. God the Father, God the Son and God the Holy Spirit. They are One, no division, no separation. When Jesus came on earth to rescue us, do you know why he called us his bride? I'm pretty sure none of us ever thought he needed a bride, but this is the only way we can partake in the affairs of the Kingdom of God. When we accept Jesus, we become a new creature; we are his bride, he is our bridegroom; we become one with Him. "*I no longer live, but Christ lives in me...*" (Galatians 2:20). Therefore, because of his Spirit dwelling inside of us, we can navigate through the various challenges life throws at us. When we are under his authority, we can recognize his Spirit within a brother or a sister, and when we become attached, we must be able to trust, not the person's character, but the Spirit of the Lord living inside. For "*Cursed is the one who trusts in man, who draws strength from mere flesh and whose heart turns*

away from the Lord [11]*."*
As you can see, we were never told to trust the man. Let's be honest, nobody is trustworthy. All people will do the same things, given the same circumstances. Jesus called us to *Love and Submit* to *Him*. And this is where many of us find it hard to obey the commands he gave both husbands and wives. We find it hard to love or submit because we either left no space in our heart for the Holy Spirit or we've just placed someone or something over him, and we wonder why the wife won't submit or why the man won't love? What is there to love? What is it that we submit to?

I am not whatsoever, implying that wives are not worthy of love or husbands worthy of respect. I am simply trying to put things into perspective. *"Submit to one another out of reverence for Christ. Wives submit yourselves to your own husbands as you do to the Lord. For the husband is the head of the wife as Christ is the head of the church, his body, of which he is the Savior. Now as the church submits to Christ, so also wives should submit to their husbands in everything.*
Husbands love your wives, just as Christ loved the church and gave himself up for her..." (Eph.5:21-25). For the relationship to work between husband and wife, there must be Christ, first and foremost. He is the example we must follow. It's His spirit that we submit to; it's His spirit of love that will flow in our life, helping us to love despite the flaws, the weaknesses or the mistakes. I can tell you how many times my husband could have or may have broken my trust over minor or major things. He could also tell you more than one thing I did that could have or may have prompted him to question his love for me. The reality is we are humans, we all make mistakes. Everyone, at some point

---
[11] Jeremiah 17:5

in their life, did things or made decisions that were greatly in contrast with the word of God. Why am I then bringing that up? Because I want us to understand that the duties assigned to husbands and wives can only flow from the relationship we have with Jesus. We learn to develop a relationship with Him – first, we get to know His voice, His word, to enjoy His presence. We learn how to trust Him even when things are in shambles. We learn how to appreciate Him for who He is, not what he does. Does this hit a nerve? I hope it does. My point here is we must learn to love our spouse for who they are, just that. I love my husband because he is my husband, not because he loves me, protects me or provides for our family. Yes, men and women both have roles to play. But we love each other because we love God. I know this is only the beginning of our journey together, but before we dive any deeper, I want us to take a moment to seek God. If you haven't accepted him as your lord and savior, you can do it just now. Tell Him with your own words that you want to know Him, tell him that He has a place in your heart, and He is welcome. Lay it all out at his feet. He will not reject you. If you have already accepted Jesus as your Lord, but you still struggle to give Him total control over your life, your health, your marriage, your finances, your children, whatever the case may be, you can still choose today to walk on a new path with Him to head in a new direction. Choose life. Just say this: Lord Jesus, let your will be done in my life.

Jesus is the only way we can make it alive in this world of chaos, confusion, and despair. He is Love, He is Light, He is Life. Because of Him, we are worthy to be loved, honored and respected.

Seek God first and all other things shall be added unto you[12]. We show our love to the Lord when we obey His commands, honor His word and submit to His Holy Spirit.

---

[12] Matthew 6:33

3
NAKED AND UNASHAMED

"*And they were both naked, the man and his wife, and were not ashamed.*" Genesis 2:25 Naked. Bare. Nude. Without clothing. Devoid of concealment or disguise. Lacking embellishment. Oh, this last phrase does sound familiar! "*He grew up before him like a tender shoot, and like a root out of dry ground. He had no beauty or majesty to attract us to him, nothing in appearance that we should desire him*[13]." Created in the image of our Lord, we also were made without embellishment. Naked. Uncovered. So, *He* could be our covering. No concealment or disguise, only his light shining through.

There was no sin, no pain, and no shame. Husband and wife living in perfect unity, open and transparent. Vulnerable and honest with each other. Trusting each other until that day when the serpent got close enough to lead them astray. He introduced them to sin, thus creating division, mistrust, and humiliation.

I've often wondered why Adam listened to Eve and ate the fruit? It was slightly difficult to imagine what may have crossed his mind at that moment. Sometimes, I feel like one of us should have shouted

---
[13] Isaiah 53:2

"is it not to you that God spoke? How did you not know Eve was being deceived?" Have you ever asked yourself the same? I guess, one may say it's irrelevant now since they already got evicted from the garden and here, we are, thousands of lights later, reaping the fruit of sin.

But this fact is very much relevant to us today. Men and women still live the aftermath of that dreadful day, casting blame upon each other, living in suspicion and defiance, fear and shame. Men blaming women for their demises, women resenting men for not holding their ground, not standing up and taking ownership. I am forced to admit I, too have been thinking something along those lines, that if Adam had not been strong enough to keep Eve in line, then it was his fault as much as it was hers...but this is not quite what happened, the Lord interjected. In fact, as I started jotting down the first lines, he said to me: "Look, this is where you all get it wrong, this is the part that most couples struggle with today." And he added: "Adam ate the fruit, not because he was weak, or being controlled by his wife, he ate because he had full confidence in her." Yes, it was wrong, by all accounts, they disobeyed God, but we cannot be oblivious to the strong bond, the deep connection they both had with each other. When one fell, the other one fell, as well. Though this is not an exhortation to sin in unison, we must understand God's intent for both husband and wife: Love, Unity, Respect, and Trust. Adam knew and trusted Eve. He understood her role, her position and knew her intentions towards him were *to bring him good and not harm*[14]. He also recognized that she was trustworthy, faithful, respectful, wise and courageous

---

[14] Proverbs 31:12

– a wife and a mother, warm and loving: The Proverbs 31 woman. And though Adam listened to his wife, the problem did not arise because man chose to listen to his wife, like many would like to argue, which turns out to be one of the many issues we face today. Communication seems to be broken between husband and wife. They both prefer to listen to everyone else around rather than taking advice from each other.

Both Adam and Eve were out of the presence of God, uncovered; and they could no longer hear and recognize his voice, they chose to listen to a voice other than the Holy Spirit of God. I wonder who else does this? Almost all of us.

God's intent was never to leave us naked and unprotected, feeling ashamed or embarrassed. His love for us was enough to cover and protect us. Our heavenly Father knew they were not perfect, never created to be all-powerful, all-knowing, but they were expected to follow and obey only him. Remember what I said before, Adam trusted the Holy Spirit within Eve and he knew she was his. They both could trust each other because their spirit could testify for each other. God's expectations are still the same today for all of us. He calls us to complete submission and total obedience to his will. Your Maker wants your heart, your love, and nothing else. *"And you shall love the* Lord *your God with all your heart, with all your soul, with all your mind, and with all your strength.' This is the first commandment[15]."* For *everything you do flows from it* [16]. Anytime we let our guards down, we subject ourselves to the treacherous lies of the enemy. We compromise God's sovereignty over our lives. We make a place in our heart for the enemy to fill. Don't we say,

---

[15] Mark 12:30 NKJV
[16] Proverbs 4:23

"*nature abhors a vacuum*"? Well, let your heart be filled with the fullness of God, and there will be no space for evil. Make your heart *his* dwelling place; *He* is big enough to fill it. Jesus wants all of you, your innermost being. Is *he* not trustworthy? When you give him your heart, you can rest assured that *he* will never leave you nor forsake you, *he* will never abandon or betray you, *he* will never reject or stop loving you. His love is everlasting. "*Know therefore that the LORD your God is God; he is the faithful God, keeping his covenant of love to a thousand generations of those who love him and keep his commandments[17]*".

Love trusts. We cannot pretend to love God and not trust him. We cannot love without knowing *Him*. There is another common mistake we often make but for now I will say this: many people claim to love God, but at the sight of the first mountain, they run and hide. Others simply have the erroneous idea that He is just a tyrant who wants to rule over our hearts and nothing more. But this could not be further from the truth. Our heavenly Father calls us to abide in Him, dwell in his presence, meditate his word, communicate with him through prayer, praise, worship, draw close to him and share one of the most intimate relationships man will ever experience. But worship requires our hearts to be open. We must accept to be honest, transparent, vulnerable, and totally naked. Naked with our feelings and emotions, our thoughts or actions, our struggles and challenges, our hopes and fears. One thing we ought to remove from our mind is the idea of someone looking down on us with a big frown and a stick in his hand, constantly seeking to catch us in the wrong. We assume that, with a disgusted look on his face, he is always on his guard, ready to throw us into the furnace. Though we may be able to grieve his Holy

---

[17] Deut. 7:9

Spirit, nothing we do will ever shock or surprise our God. He made us, He knows every single one of our thoughts before we utter the words. "*You know when I sit and when I rise; you perceive my thoughts from afar. You discern my going out and my lying down; you are familiar with all my ways. Before a word is on my tongue you, LORD, know it completely[18].*"

Keeping that in mind, let us come humbly before His throne with everything we have, failures and imperfections, without bearing the weight of shame. That's exactly the enemy's plan – to keep us wallowing in guilt, fear, and shame. But Jesus knows us inside and out, yet He gave his life for us so that we will no longer be bound to sin to truly experience the freedom to walk naked and unashamed, allowing him to touch and infiltrate every part of our being. He is the bridegroom. We are the bride. It's our moment of intimacy, but there is no intimacy without vulnerability. In that regard, Jesus calls us to act the same way with our spouse. I will never say it enough, marriage between husband and wife is meant to be a replica of our relationship with Christ. But until we fully grasp God's expectations, we will try to work something out that was never meant to exist in the first place.

Men and women were created by the same Spirit, and from the same flesh. They were never expected to become something that they never were before. In the beginning, they were one and God always expects it to remain that way. Unity is not a new concept that he threw in a jar to make things more complicated for us. This is how he made us. When we get away from God's presence, our senses become affected, we lose our sight, our hearing, we grow out of touch. We can no longer recognize that we are part of the same team,

---

[18] Psalm 139:2-4

same body. Let alone if one of us completely steps outside of God's will and starts doing the opposite of what His Word commands. We must first acknowledge that God's commandments are not a punishment; they are meant to help us on this journey, to prevent us from repeating the same errors and break the bond, the love and the trust between us. Our marital issues may not always be due to our differences or lack of this or that; it simply could be the fact that we are not properly aligned with the Word and the Spirit of the Almighty. For many years, I have struggled with back pain, I recently found out that my spine was not in the correct position, and with the help of a chiropractor, some of the displaced joints could be realigned. This is why we need Jesus in our midst; He keeps our spine right. If one or even both spouses find themselves not to be in complete alignment with the Word of God, it may lead to misunderstanding, clash and a whole lot of pain. In addition, the further we get away from the truth, the further away we get from each other. I think it would be fair to say that men and women have nothing in common except the Spirit that created them. Therefore, we can never expect to be one if we take the Holy Spirit out of the equation. By the same token, if men and women were also made from the same flesh, they are part of the same body. It is very interesting; the Bible says that God removed a rib from Adam and used it to form Eve. Can we all agree that women and men have fundamental differences, yet remain very much connected? The woman was made of what man now lacks; He lost a rib, she is that rib! I believe it is crucial for everyone to realize that we are part of the same body – same team. No competition, no adversity, if one wins; the team wins, and if one falls, everyone gets thrown out. Also, if we belong to the same body, should we feel ashamed of each other? I cannot imagine taking a shower and trying to hide my nakedness from my eyes or covering up my hand so my eyes would not see it or hiding any part of my body to the other. Sounds ridiculous, doesn't it? Well, why do married couples do the same? Why can we not be vulnerable, uncovered and feel unashamed? We should be able to get naked physically, emotionally and spiritually; naked in every aspect of our lives, without the fear of being shunned, judged, criticized, or ridiculed. What would it take for us to be open, to share our dreams, our goals, our struggles, our temptations, or shortcomings?

When we refuse to be transparent with each other, it never makes us stronger, smarter, or better. In fact, it can become very debilitating. We prevent the other person from fully utilizing every gift, ability or resource God has placed inside of them. It may take away their sense of purpose and fulfillment. Both men and women have their roles to play in the relationship. And God always joins people together with a specific purpose and neither of them are ever meant to be overlooked, overruled or overplayed. Instead, together they are called to combine both their strengths and what may be perceived as weaknesses to achieve a greater mission; bring glory to His name. The objective of being naked is to achieve total fusion, a perfect unity, where we will no longer be able to differentiate one from the other. No one will ever be able to come in between and cause dissension because will know each other from all angles. When we accept Jesus, we become a new creature. Although that simply means, from this point forward, we have a new identity; a new way of life, it also signifies that whoever sees us must see Jesus through us. We become so inextricably connected (because we abide in Him), to the point that nobody can separate. What God has joined let no man put asunder[19]. If we are crippled with shame or fear and are unable to be naked in front of each other, body, mind and soul, we leave the door open for the enemy to come in between and separate.

Therefore, I believe, shame could be translated as our fear of being uncovered or exposed. Can I say this? The world's definition of certain concepts is sometimes, if not often, at odds with God's. In the dictionary, naked means exposed, uncovered and exposed also means unprotected. Therefore, naked could be defined as being unprotected. How can we not understand why we will be haunted by the fear of being unprotected thus refusing to get completely naked, be totally vulnerable and transparent?

We are in the world, but not of it [20] and that is why we do not rely on the world's definition, understanding or methods. Instead, we stand on the Truth, which is found in the Word of God. Though we are naked and exposed, we will not be afraid. Why? Simply because our God will protect us. He is our covering. *"He will cover you with his feathers, and under his wings you will find refuge*[21]*;"* Our God is love, and we know that His love will always protect us. The only way for men to be naked and feel protected is right there, under His wings, in His presence. The only place for us to have a safe and secure relationship is under the shadow of the Almighty. He who *"dwells in the shelter of the Most High will rest in the shadow of the Almighty*[22]*"*. In His presence we shall have no fear[23] of being exposed, uncovered or unprotected. He is our protector, our defender. Furthermore, we all are also instructed to put on the armor of God, to stand against the schemes of the evil

---

[19] Mark 10:9
[20] John 17:16
[21] Psalm 91:4
[22] Psalm 91:1
[23] 2 Tim. 1:7

one[24]. This is our first and individual responsibility; to give our lives to Christ (salvation), walk on His truth, stand on His word and His righteousness, and we believe that His word is true and trustworthy and that He will never leave us. Now, as husband and wife, we also bear the responsibility to live according to God's principles, inviting His Holy Spirit to dwell in our hearts, in our lives. How is that relevant to us being naked and still be able to feel protected? Yes, some of us may not have a problem believing that God will protect us; on the other hand, we may not be able to say the same about our spouse. Are you your spouse's harshest critic? Do you tend to emphasize their flaws more often than you celebrate their strengths? Or, do you find it difficult to trust them?

Again, we find it easier to trust God because He has proven to be faithful and trustworthy; however, some couples do not have that sentiment when it comes to their spouse. Either they cannot discern the Holy Spirit at work within their spouse, or their spouse is simply not conducting themselves in a way that exemplifies Jesus.

Without a doubt, society seems more appearance-driven than ever, and it may be harder to be vulnerable. Nobody wants to feel judged or rejected. With issues such as "identity crisis," "gender neutrality," same-sex marriages, abortion rights, freedom of speech or religion and more, there is definitely a new paradigm. Many may find it more challenging to express their beliefs or their opinions. How do you find someone who can be trusted? When is it safe to share your personal struggles, to be real about your needs or desires?

First, let me say this; we may not be able to find many

---

24 Eph.6:11

people around us deserving of our trust. We may not even find that perfect friend, awesome companion, perfect spouse that will encourage us to be true to ourselves. But we find, in Jesus, the perfect reason to stop pretending. We cannot pretend to be who we are not and probably never will be. We cannot, and must not compromise our beliefs, our principles, or our expectations, simply to pacify others, satisfy our desire to "fit in" and fulfill our need for acceptance. Pastor Michael Todd of Transformation Church often addresses this topic with such resounding words, "God cannot bless who you're pretending to be". Oh, this is real! Ask Jacob! If you will stop considering your spouse as your adversary or enemy, but instead as your friend, your partner, two parts of the same body, you will become more inclined to walk in absolute honesty and transparency. You and your spouse should be able to be naked, and still feel the utmost love, respect and appreciation for each other. When we walk in the light of Christ, we are not ashamed of who we are or what we do, rather, we understand that everything we do or say is for the glory of the King. We take no part in darkness. Am I implying that we are perfect and we never make any mistakes? Absolutely not! But we make a choice daily, to be open, honest and accountable.

Marriage requires a certain level of honesty and transparency, that should neither overshadow nor compromise the love and respect we have for each other. We should never use honesty to be rude, mean, or condescending. Instead, we speak the truth in love, with the love, respect and consideration that we expect for ourselves. If the words we exchange are not guided by love, or inspired by pure motives, then we should leave it at the feet of the cross, pray about the issue until the Holy Spirit takes total control.

A man who knows the Lord understands and abides

by His rules; he seeks to honor, protect and provide for his family. He will never try to take advantage of his authority, strength or position. The same holds true for a woman who truly rests in the Lord's shadow. She will submit to the leadership of her husband, who in turn will be submitted to Christ. Now, the question is *who are you following*? Are you chasing after the myth or the truth? Appearance or reality?

PART 2

CHASING "ONENESS"

4
DATING WITH BROKEN BONES

Have you ever been denied entry to a place because of what you were carrying, or because of the person with you? Everyone carries baggage around. Some light, some heavy, but at one point we all feel the weight. What is it that you're still holding onto that may be stopping you from entering your next season? Are you afraid to move forward because of past hurt, bitterness, fear and unforgiveness? We all have stories, experiences, memories we wish we could bury or set on fire; somethings we wish would have never happened. But we can never let them deter us from reaching our destination. Let me ask you: where are you going? What are you chasing after?

Marriage today seems to be the answer to end a life of misery, loneliness and despair. Many are willing to sacrifice their dreams or aspirations and compromise their future and their values, just to wear a wedding dress and a diamond ring, to have a mile-long guest list or simply to not be alone. Others will jump from one bad relationship into another. A lot of people cannot bear the thought of being single. They love *being in a relationship* more than they actually love the person. It may not really matter who they are with as long as they're with somebody.

There is nothing wrong with loving people - we are made to love God and everyone around – but we cannot get involved with everybody. How many times will we make the same mistakes? Until we finally learn from it, right?

Men are designed to live in community, to love, care, protect, provide, all these different things. But just like the Ecclesiastes taught us there's a time and a season for everything[25]. Every person is unique, with specific needs, desires and a purpose to fulfill. And I believe our Creator places people in our lives at different times, different seasons, for various reasons. When we don't understand this, when we are clueless about our own identity in Christ Jesus, or our mission here on Earth, it can be very difficult to be with the right person. In fact, what will we use as gauge to determine whether the person is right for us? Besides, this is how many of us end up with either the wrong person, in the wrong type of relationship, or even with the right person, at the wrong time. This last statement might make you raise your eyebrow. But read this: *"Promise me, O women of Jerusalem, not to awaken love until the time is right.*[26]" As you can see, there is a time for love to awaken. But we will discuss this in a later chapter.

Love and release

The Lord gave me this imagery very recently. I saw a woman taking care of wounded birds. She will take them in, clean up their wounded wings, feed them, then she would release them. But she would never keep them. I had no idea what that meant. Then, the Lord said to me: "I've placed, in the heart of women, incredible gifts and talents; they're able to love without limitations, their hearts can stretch further than they would ever think. Not only can they love and nurture others, they can also share the gift of love; they are life

---

[25] Ecclesiastes 3
[26] Song of Solomon 8:4

bearers, life givers. And because of this, they will always attract wounded birds." At that point, I went from clueless to being confused. I still didn't understand the bird metaphor, or the link between love and the birds, until *He* added; "Always be clear about the reason why the birds come, why I allow them to come into your life. For I send them so they can receive life again, for you to nurture and feed them; but know they're not yours to keep." Need a translation?

A woman meets a guy and they will have a terrific connection. As their friendship evolves, she begins to see the man's weaknesses, areas of hurt, trauma, pain, or hopelessness. She will find herself able to bring a smile on his face, hope in his life. Instead of releasing him, they will become romantically involved. What's wrong with this picture? The woman does exactly what she is supposed to do: feed, nurture and care, but she is not clear about the nature of their relationship. She doesn't know the reason why God sent the man. But instead of seeking, asking, checking with Him, she assumes the man is hers to keep. She therefore gives more than what she was ever supposed to give, expects more than she was supposed to receive, and becomes more attached than she should have been. The bird was not hers to keep. She was supposed to love and release. Feed, nurture, clean the wounds and release. Had she asked the Father who knows all things, she would have heard this: "I brought him to you in his season of brokenness, loneliness, confusion and hopelessness, so that you could love him like a brother, a friend, or even like a child, to point him back to Me, feed him with My words, not your body. Love him, don't fall in love."

But when we don't dare to ask God before doing anything, and before making any decision, we may become attached to the wrong person or even fall in love with someone else's husband. Before we know it, we start making excuses as to why the person came into our life, flirting with the idea of a possible future together. I will not go into much detail here, but let me say this, our Lord is the God of order; though you may be confused as to why He allowed your paths to cross, He is never the author of confusion, chaos and disorder. There is a difference between love and sex. You can love someone without becoming emotionally, physically or sexually attached. We've had or still have friends in our life that God sent for a season, for the purpose of us loving them, encouraging and building them up. Not all relationships end in marriage.

How do we know when to love and release, or when to love and keep? It all comes down to having a relationship with the Father. Trusting His plan for our lives. Being patient enough to wait until He takes us into the promised land. Moreover, we cannot forget that there is always a transition season, a wilderness moment, as God never takes us out of one place straight into the next. I read a blog recently, and the author brilliantly stated that with God it's always these three words: "out, through and in".

God takes us *out* of one place, situation, condition *through* a journey *into* the next season. Don't ever confuse your "through", season with your "in" season. Very often, we meet people who look almost everything like what we desire. They fit almost to perfection the criteria we've established for ourselves, and because we see what we like or think we need, because our emotions are high, we are mistaken, and we start building tents which may look like homes to us, right there in the wilderness. We settle in a place that we were only meant to cross through. We chase after things or people who were never ours to have. And we either blame God for our failed attempts or we

"force" Him to be a part of a story He's never written. Yes, you were never designed to be a couple! You had a mission in each other's life, to either learn a valuable lesson, bring you into the next chapter of your life, or hold your hand while you went through various life challenges. Some people are just like a bridge; they help us cross over, connect some dots, but as corny as it may sound, if we cannot park a vehicle on a bridge, neither can we make them become our partners for life. Our primary calling as a Christian is to "Go and make disciples", bring back the lost, the backslidden. God will send us to people who find themselves at a crossroad. Though He uses any situation to rescue His lost sheep, He never does it to our detriment. But the key is to invite the Holy Spirit to dwell in our heart, to guard it and protect us from giving or expecting more than we should. The Lord also reminded me of the story of Saul, when he went out looking for his father's donkeys (1 Samuel 9). And He said: "whether it's the donkeys, the birds or the man, they all belong to Me."
We must therefore abide in Him, stay in perfect alignment with *His* will, *His* vision and *His* plan. When we have the wrong perception or the wrong understanding of God's expectations and His work through us, it may cause us to stumble and fall, get acquainted with the wrong people or get us to build a nest for people who were only supposed to pass us by.

Broken compass

A compass helps us to find our direction or orientation. The Holy Spirit is the one and only compass Christians can and must rely on to help them navigate through our journey here on Earth. Not only does He know where we start and where we are going, He also knows the "how" and the "why". He has the entire script in His hand. He even knows us inside and out, so He is not unaware of our strengths, abilities, or our limitations. All we need to do is to listen, trust and follow. Additionally, life has its way of teaching us lessons we sometimes judge unnecessary. We would rather take turns that we feel will be best for us, even when the red light keeps flashing in front of us. How many of us have made the unilateral decision to recalculate our route? We've concluded that our Holy Spirit map was defective, or the route seemed too long, and we just could not follow or wait anymore. News alert! The enemy has not left the battlefield. His plan is still the same, to cause you to doubt God and create your own path. Can I tell you, anything you build without God, any route you follow where He does not lead, is bound to fail and lead you to destruction? Unless the Lord builds the house, they labor in vain who build it." (Psalm 127:1).

The enemy will trick and misguide you, make you feel impatient and doubtful. He tries to blur and saturate your line of communication with the Father, to take you into a ditch. Just like he did with the first man and the first woman, the enemy will do it again with you, unless you take a different approach. Follow God and trust the Holy Spirit. His route may be long, but it is the safest and the only way to Heaven. What happens when we lose our connection with the Lord? What happens when we let our emotions dictate our actions? What happens when we listen to our own voice or the enemy's, instead of listening to God's words, when we take shortcuts instead of following the Holy Spirit's long route, or when we can no longer hear from Him anymore? We make incorrect assumptions, wrong decisions, costly mistakes, which take us on a steep road to hurt, pain and disappointment; drowning in a pool of shame, guilt and regrets. We further convince ourselves that this was God's will, our loving Father's plan. Many would claim that God simply wanted us to learn from those mistakes, to go through the heartache and the heartbreak. But let me tell you God's plan is never to leave you with a broken heart! Yes, He will mend your broken heart but His will is to guard your heart and prevent it from being broken. It is time that we become accountable for our own decisions. We cannot continue to make poor decisions and expect God to take the fault, just like we cannot make informed decisions from a place of hurt and brokenness. One may ask: but why then, did God let me fall for this person, if He knew it wasn't going to work? Because His goal is to draw you closer to Him. If He couldn't make you come to Him before (because God never forces anything on us), He will be patient enough to wait for you to come back. When are we going to realize that He is Alpha, the beginning of all things? When are we going to reach a point in our relationship where we will not make a single decision without seeking first His counsel and guidance? Did you not realize that the whole thing was just about you and God? All relationships draw from the one we have with our Maker. Don't try to build a life with someone or mend a relationship with anyone without first working on your Father-Child relationship (God the Father), bridegroom-bride relationship (Christ the Husband). This is how it begins.

Too many of us have had abandonment or rejection issues stemming from an inconstant relationship with our mother or father, trust issues due to cheating or abuse from previous relationships, divorce. Many suffer from low or no self-esteem, emotional oppression, emotional dependence, fear of loneliness, fear to love and trust again, fear of losing someone we love, fear of failure, or other insecurities. Whatever the issues may be, they usually find their root in the perception we have of ourselves, the definition and the expectations we set when it comes to love and relationship.

Again, it's all about the knowledge we have of God, the trust we place in Him and our willingness to reciprocate the love He has for us. Understanding that no marriage, no relationship can thrive apart from His presence.

Knowing God, Accepting yourself

Jesus is calling us into a deeper level of trust and intimacy. I am reminded of the Apostle Peter walking on the water[27]. Why would Jesus, in the middle of the night, ask him to walk on water? What is it that Peter could not see on dry ground?

There comes a time in our walk with the Lord when separation will be required; not just from the familiarity of those around us, but from the comfort of our natural environment. The further we get from our comfort zone, the more we will be required to trust God. Walking on water, for us Christians, is not a physical activity to try, it's a movement of the Spirit to stretch our faith. Most importantly, it takes us to another level of knowing God. How will walking on water help us know God a little more?

If we have family or friends by our side, it's easy to be distracted. We may be tempted to rely or depend on them. But when we face situations that are meant to take us away from the familiar into the unknown, from the safe to the uncertain, from the natural into the supernatural – situations that force us to let go of what

---

[27] Matthew 14:22-29

we can control or anything we can hold on to – the only way we can make it alive is by keeping our eyes on Jesus, the author and finisher of our faith. What's more interesting is the disciples never knew Jesus could do such a thing; walking on water, they even thought they were seeing a ghost. But as soon as they saw Peter walking towards Him, and they both eventually climbed back into the boat, they all learned something new about their Master. Indeed, they exclaimed: *"You really are the Son of God!"*. Why is this relevant to marriage and our relationship with God? Peter obtained the revelation of who Jesus is, and was given the keys to Heaven, he was recognized as the rock on which the Church will be established. How will Peter trust that word unless he saw what Jesus was able to do? For we cannot enter covenant with anyone unless we know who they are. You cannot follow where God is taking you, unless you accept who He says you are. When Peter witnessed that Jesus is the Son of God, who can stand upon the waters, calm the raging seas, do you think he could not believe that the same Jesus will be able to make him the rock of His church, like He promised? God calls us to not rely on our own understanding, our wisdom, our strength, but to fully lean and trust in Him. There's a place He wants to take you, a place where no one else is allowed. He is a jealous God, He will not share His glory with a man. If we're not willing to strip ourselves naked, get rid of everyone or everything around us that provides safety, comfort, or "happiness"; we've set ourselves up to fail, by not placing them before God.

By this statement alone, "I the Lord your God am a jealous God" (Exodus 20:5), and throughout the scriptures, we can rightly affirm that God is monogamous. He takes us as His bride and expect us to love Him, consecrate ourselves to Him, honor worship and praise Him, living a life that pleases Him and no others. We cannot and should not make our life revolve around a person.

Anyone who believes they need a husband or a wife to complete them, make them whole, bring joy or even give sense to their life is robbing God of His place, His power and is denying the sacrifice He paid to bring us back into His covenant. Know the Lord your God and don't be afraid to go alone to have a one on one meeting with Him. It's not like you are being called into the principal's office for a correction. He wants your full, undivided attention. Not to chastise you, not to keep you prisoner, but to teach you everything you need to know as His bride. He wants to show and give you the keys to access His Kingdom. It's hard, almost impossible to have a fulfilling relationship with someone you don't know. Take the time to know God, develop a relationship with Him through prayer and worship, by reading His word.

In the beginning of this chapter, I asked what are you chasing after? Is it the ceremony, the ring, the status, the position? Do you want the man, or the woman more than you want God?

You may not know who you are, but God knows. You may not know how to love yourself; thus, you may be seeking love from every angle possible, seeking men's approval and acceptance, willing to give yourself to everyone who's able to make you feel like you matter. But these are lies form the enemy, to keep you in bondage and prevent you from experiencing the deep, pure, fulfilling, satisfying love the Father has for you. You are called to walk in the truth, which includes understanding, accepting every flaw, weakness and shortcoming. For they all make your story worthwhile. You are special in the eyes of the Lord. Every lesson, every experience, every disappointment, every failure reveals the ultimate love God has for you. And until you accept the truth of who God says you are, you will never be able to walk in freedom, live your purpose and bring glory to the Father. You cannot believe everything people say, while denying what your Creator says about you.

Your broken bones were never meant to keep you in pain, to stop you from moving or to keep you on the ground; they are only a beautiful reminder of the grace, the love and the mercy of our Savior. He always gives us more than one chance to start over. Although His will is to see us succeed on the first try, it doesn't matter how many times we fall, but it matters how many times we choose to get up and continue.

God wants you to not only get up, but to hold your hands every time you get up, to help you walk, run, jump, shout. Stay strong till the end. Strength is not measured by the mistakes you avoid, the right man or woman you can find; your strength is found in your ability to trust and depend on God, in the midst of your trials.

5
TOO LOW, TOO HIGH

It wasn't supposed to be this way! This was never supposed to happen! Why is it that we are always encouraged, or told to clearly set our boundaries, define our expectations, yet every time we do so, we end up getting upset, frustrated, disappointed or hurt? What barometer (what standards), are we using to set those expectations when it comes to love and relationships? Many of us grew up reading or watching fairy tales; those perfect ending stories about *Sleeping Beauty* or *Cinderella* – falling in love with the handsome charming prince and living happily ever after with their many children. This introduced us for the first time to the notion of love and marriage. Subconsciously, we too embark on this life journey, chasing after the same ideals – the happily ever after. We begin our quest to find our prince charming, or our Cinderella, oblivious to the fact that life is nothing like a fairy tale. In fact, life is never smooth sailing; it has many bumpy roads. It's not that we should not have dreams and goals, but are we setting ourselves up to fail, right from the start, due to unrealistic expectations? Are our lists too long or are they way too short?

How often do we enter a marriage covenant without being clear on our hopes, dreams and aspirations? How many of us have had expectations in our heads that were never expressed, but assumed our spouse will prove himself to us by guessing the correct answer? Right from the start, we pin a list long of unreasonable demands, wants and needs that not a single person would be able to fulfill. We design in our minds, a picture of our dream relationship, and hope to see it come to pass with a single brushstroke. Unfortunately, life is not an abstract painting. We have been assigned a specific purpose, therefore, we must be intentional in everything we do or say. Yes, it's very important, even crucial to define boundaries and set clear expectations, but we cannot, unilaterally, plan out our entire life with someone. It takes two to tango. "*Can two people walk together without agreeing on the direction[28]?*" (Amos 3:3). Walking in agreement suggests that we clearly enunciate our goals, hopes and expectations. Marriage is not a guessing game. We must take the time to learn about each other, our vision, mission, strength and weakness, stories and life experiences, challenges and struggles.

The D- Myth

What happens when we start a business without a business plan, enter into a contract without understanding the terms of the agreement? We are doomed to fail or make mistakes that could have been avoided. Marriage is by far the most important decision one could ever make in life. The choice of a life partner is not to be taken lightly. But how can we make such a life changing decision without getting the proper information? Athletes or soldiers always train, get ready before going into the field. Of course, Marriage is neither a game nor a war, but we do have an adversary, who is cunning, relentless, determined to come between us and create dissension, chaos and division. From the day we were created, he vowed to

---

[28] New Living Translation

destroy every good thing God has given us and that includes our love life, our relationship with God and with others. The enemy is after every seed God planted in us. We cannot and we must not continue to ignore his schemes and tactics. Therefore, we believers, can no longer refuse to address the D-word, and I am not talking about Divorce. Yes, we want to take a stand against divorce for God hates it, but if we took the time to learn and educate ourselves more about marriage, if we became more familiar with God's expectations about marriage, we will be more equipped for it and less inclined to even consider divorce as an option. We so vehemently chose the latter that now, we are even afraid to use any word starting with the same letter.

D- Dating. Why should we remain silent when it comes to premarital relationships? The enemy's plan is to make us feel wrong about dating and courtship, and unfortunately this seems to be working. Too many people are falling in the trap, and the consequences have been simply catastrophic, worse than the things we were trying to avoid. Now, because marriage is becoming an illusion, a lie, or a fantasy; less and less people even believe in the possibility of having a healthy and Holy relationship. Why should we continue to turn a blind eye? Can we afford to remain silent in the face of the perversion and the defilement that is happening in our communities, our cities, in every nation?

Christians are being misled and misinformed when it comes to love, marriage and relationships. Too many choose not to address the things that seem to cause the most damage. If only we could make something disappear by not talking about it, but we know too well, that will never happen. Most of us want to get it right, we thirst for the correct information, the right path to walk on, but all we have is the information that the world provides, because they are the only one to speak about dating and sexuality. Those purulent dating websites, which have nothing Christian about them except the name, are the perfect traps. Most are wolves dressed in sheep's clothing coming to lure and trick us into fornication, adultery or other kinds of sin. Where do you go, who do you turn to when you are looking to abide in God's truth, walk according to His precepts and commands? How do you find the right, biblical answers to your questions? What's the proper way for a Christian to go about meeting someone and deciding to join their life forever? How many bad marriages can we afford to have, some of which should have never been celebrated in the first place had they only received the proper information? How many more families can we watch be destroyed? When do we break the silence and start teaching and training our young boys and girls about the sanctity of marriage, how to embrace their sexuality while remaining in the will of the Father? How do we get them ready for marriage? We've talked about the don'ts for so long that we forgot to teach them about the do's, and they grow up with the desire to do something, live in something they were never prepared for. It looks like a room everyone sees, but no one can open the door. Nobody knows what's behind, until the day one is "of age" and is thrown inside. Now it will be up to them to figure out how to navigate through the various challenges. Does it not sound familiar? The Tree of Knowledge of Good and Evil. Men touched exactly what was strictly prohibited. The same thing is happening, and we must do it differently this time.

Oh, how much easier it would have been if they had been taught everything, they needed to know about being a husband or being a wife! Instead, we learn

from television, social media, or other secular outlets.
Many marriages break apart because of infidelity or pornography, among others. The problem is that we try to set adults free from sexual immorality when we could have trained teenagers about the biblical way to live out their sexuality. Most men or women addicted to pornography today did not start when they got married; many were already exposed early on, but had no way of learning about the ramifications, the impact it would have on their lives. The same way we are introduced to the concept of love through fairy tales, is the same way young boys and girls learn about sexuality through adult movies or magazines, and this is what they are: myths and lies. Therefore, we cannot expect anyone to act or be the same way as what we saw in these "materials".

We still have the time and opportunities to rectify and to recalibrate. We have victory through Christ Jesus and the truth will set us free, but who will teach the truth? We all have the responsibility to learn, get the proper information and pass it on to those coming behind us. *"My people are destroyed from lack of knowledge."* (Hosea 4:6). And therefore, we cannot stress enough the absolute necessity to develop an intimate relationship with God. He is the most reliable source of information. He is the Omniscient One, and not only will He teach us, but He will also give us the revelation of His word. When your car or any other piece of machinery or equipment is defective, they usually refer you to the manufacturer. The same holds true for our God. He is the Creator, who knows right from wrong, the truth from the lies, the original from the counterfeit. Another mistake we make in our pre-marriage season is to rush things out for the sake of getting married. And we proudly rely on the Apostle

Paul "*it is better to marry than to burn with passion.[29]*" to provide the perfect excuse or give us good conscience. Though I am by no means advocating for living together without marriage, I am not either a proponent to rushing into getting married.

Is there a right time?

The easy answer will be yes, for the Bible says there is a time for everything, meaning there is a right time to do a thing. But how do we know when the time is right? Who even sets that time? I cannot pretend to have the answer to this question. All I can say we usually know when something is not right.
The most important thing is; nobody should get married for the wrong reasons. The Apostle Paul was not encouraging us to get married for the sake of not burning. Marriage was not to solve our inability to control our sexual impulses. In fact, he understood what a serious responsibility husband and wife both share in such a covenant, because he was living his life completely devoted to God and could probably not fathom the idea to have to do the same for another human being (emphasis mine). Marriage is too serious of a commitment to be taken lightly. Though we may not know if there is a right time, we know more than one reason why someone should not get married.
Too often, we hear or witness the story of people whose relationship could have made all of us drool, fall apart in the most shocking ways. They may have started in what seemed like the perfect circumstances, because they did not take the time to discuss the most important issues, lay out the proper foundations for their marriage to succeed or sometimes simply got

---
[29] 1 Corinthians 7:9

married for the wrong reasons (to relinquish their single life like an old worn out garment), but they cannot find a way to overcome the tests and trials along the way. Their "mood compatibility", physical attraction or sexual chemistry could no longer do the bidding. Or we "settle" with the person who seems to check the most out of our checkbox, or at least is the closest to our ideal spouse.

From the day you meet someone until the day you say, "I do", the work already starts. It should not be time wasted on finding out whether they like cereal or toast for breakfast, it's not the time to be obsessed about a wedding date, the dress or the number of bridesmaids, either, but to carefully consider and align your views on serious questions. This is the time to date, not according to the world standards, but in a way that pleases and glorifies God. Finding out about the other person's morals and values, beliefs and vision. As I already mentioned, learn about their stories and life experiences, family dynamics, red, green yellow, all the potential flags that may require your attention. Do you share the same values or beliefs? Where do they see themselves one, two or five years from now? Do they want a family? Do they believe in marriage? Will they ever consider divorce if things don't go the way they anticipate? How do they feel about this or that? Serious questions that could potentially make it sink or swim. Who are their friends? What qualities do they seek in a spouse? Many topics should be discussed during that time, not to check a list but to truly assess the challenges or opportunities ahead. Above all, we seek God first. What is God revealing to you concerning the person? Remember the wounded bird? Is this someone that God is sending only for a season to help you cross over or is this the person you should marry?

Being single should not be the only requirement to

start dreaming about a future with someone, because they may physically be single but unavailable emotionally. They may be all that you ask of God in a man or a woman, and yet they're not be yours. They may even be yours but still need to work on themselves first as individuals. The mistake we often make, especially women, is to meet a person and make them a "project". We see their flaws and automatically, our maternal instinct kicks in and we feel like it's our responsibility to save them, rescue them or even show them how much love we can offer. We become more involved than we should have been, get closer than we should have and fall harder than we were supposed to., only to realize a few months or even years later the terrible mistake we made. Even when we have the certitude to have met the right one, even when everything points to him, or we get confirmation from many witnesses; it never gives us license to put the cart before the horse. You can be engaged, that will still not give you the right to have sex. How many times did we see people break off their engagement? The only time sex between two people is not a sin, is under the covenant of marriage, not the simple promise of marriage.

Your body, God's temple

When I met my husband, I had no doubt about the reason why he was in my life. We received confirmation from more than one witness, had many words from the Lord and so forth. The way the Lord will use us during our prayer gatherings, was incredible. Two halves of the same fruit. We got carried away and thought it was not such a big deal whether we waited marriage to have sexual intercourse. So, we did, I became pregnant with our first son. Before I could tell that I was pregnant, the Lord impressed on my heart to take a 3-day Esther Fast. During my times of devotion and prayer, the scriptures I would always receive were all related to chastisement and childbirth pain. By day 2, I suspected I was pregnant. I knew the feeling because I had a child before and the symptoms were very similar. On the last day, close to the time to break the fast, I took a pregnancy test and just like I suspected; I was pregnant! I lived a very stressful and painful pregnancy. I had an open cervix and was placed on bed rest by week 20. There was no confusion in my mind as to why I was going through this hurdle – I was living in sin. God was not letting me have it because at every prayer meeting, from every word of knowledge, even when He spoke through me, it always had a reference to sexual immorality and sanctification. It was a Sunday morning, I was eight months pregnant, getting ready to go to Church, I could not stop singing the song "I surrender", had no idea why until I got to church. What do you think the message was about? Surrender! At the end of the preaching, the pastor asked the congregation – it was a very small church in Maryland – to declare publicly the things we chose to surrender. There I was with my pregnant belly, hearing the words come out of my mouth, words I knew did not come from me; "I surrender fornication". After I utter the words, I barely had time to think about it, the pastor started to clap and invited the entire congregation to come around and give me a hug. Apparently, it was a bigger deal than I thought. That day, I realized not only how much God loved me, but to what extent He will go for me; great lengths He will take, methods He will use, and every setting to draw me back to Him, and keep me in His will. My husband missed the episode, He was working in Delaware at the time, so after I had told Him what happened, He was informed of my decision to follow through with what I had publicly confessed at Church. And so it remained, until we got married after the birth of our son. Why am I telling this story? Because the Lord wants me to, and like I said earlier, this book is not written with a desire to judge or condemn anybody. I cannot encourage you to walk in the truth while hiding my own. I am no better, no different than anyone. I made a lot of mistakes and learned a great deal from it. And if God allowed me to overcome, learn and make better decisions, if my mistakes can prevent you from doing the same, or encourage many of you to stay on track, it would have been worth the embarrassment. It is all for the glory of God. I also shared our story to highlight what a strong position our God has on sexual purity, sanctification and holiness. Isn't He the Holy One? We are made in His image, to live the same way. I have seen people, who were destined to be together have their union delayed, postponed, challenged because they did not walk in purity. It's such an open door for the enemy to come in, and try to avert God's plan. I don't want any of you to remain fixated on the "don't" in my testimony or anything I stated concerning sex before marriage. If anything, I want you to appreciate how valuable you are in God's eyes. Your body is His temple. And He wants you to keep it pure not because sex is immoral or repulsive (like some argue, just to scare you or dissuade you), but because the only context sexual relations find their meaning. is in the sacred covenant of marriage; between man and woman. The same way, you never want to get married because of sex!

Wedding or Marriage?

If sex is not a valid reason to get married, the idea of a

magnificent wedding cannot be one either. Some people just love the idea of being in love. It doesn't really matter who they end up with as long as they are not alone. They assume being with someone will somehow make their life easier. In today's culture, marriage is reduced to the wedding day. The ceremony and the reception supersede everything else. We invest more time and money into wedding planning than we do planning our future together. All the important questions are left in the back seat, up until we face real life challenges. While most have a pretty accurate understanding about weddings, very few are prepared to deal with the demand and the pressure of marriage. Leaving father and mother, leaving prior hurt, disappointment, failure behind, coming together as one, blending ideas, habits, styles, vision and dreams require way more than a wedding planner and some designing skills. It takes more than living under one roof, we must learn how to love someone as we love ourselves, respect and honor them, provide and care for them in a way we were never required before. Marriage is not the fairy tale we grew up imagining it would be, we face serious issues, disappointments and disillusion. Marriage is a very personal affair, just like your relationship with the Lord is personal. It is the beginning of a new adventure with someone, while being the continuity of your love relationship with the Lord.

Is marriage the end?

When we talk about expectations, we often miss the mark because we consider marriage as either the end of our troubles, our loneliness, our suffering, or we perceive it as an achievement, an accomplishment. Either way, our perspective will have a profound impact on how we approach it. We reduced marriage to wearing a ring and have made it seem like it's our only expectation of a man. You like it, you put a ring on it and that's the end of it.

If you wait for a husband to make you whole, feel complete or worth something; you are in for a rude awakening. God made woman to be the man's helpmate. He said it wasn't good for man to be alone (Genesis 2:18); God never mentioned either one being incomplete. We have the wrong belief that a woman is not complete until she finds a husband. As a matter of fact, I believe we are intentionally misled by the enemy of our soul. This is an outright lie of the devil that leads to a generation of broken women. Women who are being stigmatized because they are not married. We make them feel like a failure, as if they were inadequate. Yes, women have an innate need to love and nurture. This need is simply in accordance with their call to give life. It should never be taken as a manufacturing defect, to deny women their tremendous role and place in God's Kingdom. Women are still men's helpmate whether married or single. The idea that their help is limited to a marital relationship could not be more absurd. Marital status is not indicative of someone's value, therefore, whether you choose to remain single or answer God's call to marriage will not take away the value you have in His eyes. It will not void the purpose for which He created you. Don't you ever feel the need to get with someone because you are afraid to be alone or because of shame or out of embarrassment. Marriage is not the end of a person's life. It's only the beginning of a new chapter, one that some may choose to never experience and they cannot be chastened for their choice. However, let's remember, whether you choose to be in a marital relationship with someone, you are first and foremost called into a covenant relationship with Jesus. You are *His* bride. Every relationship we form in this life must be done in accordance with His principles. We cannot reinvent the wheel. If we try to make it based on our own understanding, rely on our perspective, opinion or our own will; we will end up hurt and broken. Our Creator knows what we need, He knows the appropriate limit, the right measure. Let us align our views with His, set our expectations to reflect His will. "Unless *the Lord builds the house, the builders labor in vain*" (Psalm 127:1) Indeed, anything you try to build without relying on God first, will not last; it will dissipate like vapor.

6
NO STRINGS ATTACHED

Who does not like a bargain? How many of us think a meal always tastes better when you are not paying the bill? Do we not like the idea of "buy now pay later"? The only problem is we get the car, the house or anything else, but when comes the time to pay, that item no longer looks very appealing – buyer's remorse? If we could find a way not to pay or return the merchandise, many will certainly do just that and this is the way we live, or have been living for decades. People get into relationships with the same mentality; nobody wants to commit! In today's culture, "open" or "casual" relationships are becoming the norm. We must keep our options open they say, don't they say you should not place all your eggs in one basket also? Should this rule even apply to relationships between male and female? Is it the model we are called to abide by, the standard by which one must live his life?

Living together

If there is no absolute evidence to suggest that cohabitation before marriage increases the risks of divorce, there is nothing to support the contrary, either. However, many couples argue this is the best way to get a foretaste of what married life would be. They want to *test the waters before diving in*, assuming it will provide them with a better understanding of what to expect. So, they move in together, with the hope of getting married someday. Until it happens, they fail to realize the only thing they really share are a bed, the bills, and a few memories.

There is no real commitment, no attachment. This situation not only creates a false sense of security; it robs us of the reality of a covenant life with someone. Living together is a smaller decision to make compared to the big "I do". This is why it's so attractive, and why it works for a lot of people. There is no way out in marriage, –or at least, in God's design– it is a lifetime commitment, a promise to not only love, honor and respect, but to protect, provide and support for the rest of your life. There is an element that we tend to forget when we talk about cohabitation; the level of commitment, the willingness to fight till the end. But then again less and less people want to bear the responsibility to care for someone other than themselves. They will be willing to share what they have with someone else, if they see the return on their investment. They will not relent at the idea of splitting everything in half.

What has been will be again

Everybody wants to enjoy the benefits of marriage without carrying the responsibility. We want the blessings but reject the one who blesses. Is this not what we do with our Lord? We ask for His promises, protection, provision, but refuse His presence. We want Him to speak into our situation, move mountains on our behalf but we can't make time in your busy schedule to talk to Him in prayer.

Why am I connecting the two? Because they are so inextricably linked. How often do we hear "we live in a post Christian society", or there is a paradigm shift? We cannot be blindfolded by what's happening. If someone is considered insane for doing the same things over and over but expect a different result, then we might as well call ourselves insane. The culture of the world today to indulge in pleasures of the flesh, paganism, idolatry, perversion or sexual immorality is not something new. Homosexuality, adultery or fornication are not "new" sins. Remember Sodom and Gomorrah? The adulterous woman or the Samaritan woman living with a man who was not her husband? What makes us think what happened then will not happen now? Is God not the same for the years to come? Has He changed? Men may "update" the definition of the word *sin*, or our perception of reality may falter, but our Lord is the Holy one.

Society is not said to be "post Christian" because sin "suddenly" made its entrance; we have chosen to evolve with the world, instead of upholding the truth of the Word of God. We have deliberately made the decision to retreat and let the world have its way. The Church of the golden calf. We cannot wait for Moses to come back, so we build our own god, can't wait for Isaac, so we settle with Ismael, cannot endure submission to our leaders so we leave and start our own Church. We cannot wait for the wedding, so we live together while we "wait", can't wait for the husband, so we have a baby on our own. It's easy to assume that technology and the likes are causing such disastrous consequences, but we, believers, cannot be duped. Everything we see in the world today is a replica of what happened with the people of God. The behavior today could not be more like what they did. Also, we cannot be misled to believe we can duplicate or exude the same behaviors (with only minor variations) and have a different outcome. Will the same cause not produce the same effect? What makes us believe the same God who destroyed the cities of

Sodom and Gomorrah cannot, or will not do the same today?

Fear to commit, slave to the ideal

In the previous chapter, we addressed the unreasonable expectations we have placed on marriage. Whether too low or too high, they can cost us more than what we are willing to pay or can afford to pay. There seems to be such an imbalance between the expectations placed on women versus men. Today, a lot of women fall under the pressure, or the lie of the enemy I must say; to live up to a standard that God never set for them while acting in complete disregard for the rules He has established. Women are expected to meet certain requirements; they must pass multiple tests to determine whether they are "wife material". We begin a relationship with the erroneous notion that the woman carries the weight of the relationship. They must do everything to make it work. They must be beautiful, smart, know how to cook and clean, great in bed, but they must also be financially independent i.e. have a job or a successful career. They must be caring and loving but not get too attached. They must be giving, but not too demanding. They must oversee the house but remain quiet when the man does not act right. They must act like the wife but not expect the commitment. Some may not ask everything I mentioned, but we know it's very close. The problem is not because men expect all these things from women. The problem is that women have accepted to lower their standards, they have accepted to devalue themselves. They are willing to make all kinds of sacrifice and compromise just for a ring or a status and as soon as they get married, they want to change everything. Suddenly, they find their voice and want to claim their identity. One thing leading to another, they find themselves sitting in court, feeling betrayed, abused, hurt and broken. If we don't realize that marriage is not a reward for "passing the test", if we simply can't understand that there is not even "a test" that we, women should subject ourselves to, we will also fail to walk in the freedom that Christ set before us. The notion that it's the woman who must make a man want to marry her could not be more absurd. If a man cannot see any reasons to marry you, other than because he needs a maid, a meal, a warm bed or someone to care for his kids, then you may want to think again about the kind of man you wish to live with for the rest of your life. By the same token, no man should make you feel so desperate that you see no other way than to sleep or live in his house before he calls you his officially, his before God and before men. Stop carrying your single self as if it was a dead weight you couldn't wait to dump on the first person who starts talking to you. We all know what love is, but let's not forget what love is not. Love is not something you can force; love is a choice and love is a decision! Therefore, you cannot make that choice for someone else. You can't make someone love you, you can't force someone to make you their wife. If you do, you may get the ring, but you never get their heart. They may share their bed, but they will never share their life. They may call you their wife, but they will never treat you as such. If you cannot see your value, if you don't recognize whose you are, no man will ever change that. Our identity is not found in men; it is found in Jesus Christ. If you need a man to feel confident and important, it may simply mean you haven't yet embraced the word of God; you haven't spent enough time in His presence. For He is the only one who will never get tired of reminding you how precious you are, how loved you are, how important you are. He will not just say it, He will prove it. As a matter of fact, He's already proved Himself to you long ago, on the cross of Calvary. If our Lord Jesus, our Bridegroom paid the price before He even got His bride, why should we women let men use and abuse us without any real commitment? Why are we allowing them to "test drive" before they make the purchase? And I am not even implying that we are merchandise, but since this is the saying, I only want us to understand the dangerous path we are taking. Women are life givers, I cannot stress this enough. This means God gave us the power to bring life over our circumstances, our society, our communities, everything in and around us. If we fully grasp the implications of this statement, things will work differently. Men can only do what women are willing to accept. They will only take what we are willing to offer. (I am not discounting rape, molestation, or abuse; I am referring to the way God intended, in consensual relationships). The same way nobody will ever go to the bank trying to withdraw money from an account they never deposited any money into, is the same way women must not allow men to rip the benefits of marriage when they refuse to enter the covenant of marriage. Why should we feed into their narrative that you must prove yourself first?

Women should not be put to the test! They should not seek to honor some imaginary vows that were never pronounced, while men run around putting their fingers on everything that moves.

In my culture we have a saying, "if you sell yourself cheap, they will buy you on credit". Americans may not see anything wrong with it, since credit cards are the preferred method of payment. But, in Africa, at least in French speaking countries, we buy everything cash, there's not even a credit card system, everything is debit. In other words, this means, they will never pay! Look at the average credit card debt in America. We know that most people will not pay their credit card debts when given the opportunity or pay just the minimum.

The time has come now, for women to take back their power, reclaim what is rightfully theirs and live according to God's principles.

PART 3

DEFILING "ONENESS"

7
WHAT ABOUT LOVE?

Today there is no difference between Christian and secular marriage. We apply worldly wisdom to a Godly institution, hoping we can have the best of both worlds. We want a religious wedding, a godly marriage, but refuse to abide by God's principles. It's easier to follow the rules that society has imposed on us. Marriage is to make you happy, therefore if you are unhappy, you have the absolute right to call it quits. This is how marriages have been destroyed and families ripped apart.
The world tells us you don't have to stay committed if you don't feel like it. If things don't work out the way you anticipated, you are entitled to walk out without ever looking back. If you're feeling a little bored and need to spice things up, you can invite someone else in your bed. The world also claims that marriage should be an unending story of love, romance, hugs and kisses. The only part they omit is to tell you that this is a fallacy. This kind of relationship is not real and was never meant to be called marriage. They say marriage should never make you shed a tear, never make you cry, never cause you any inconvenience or sacrifice. It should meet all your expectations and fulfill all your dreams. Therefore, if it doesn't, you should end it and find the one that will. I certainly would have agreed if marriage was a game, a toy, a movie, a song or just a thing. However, it's not! I would have also agreed if

marriage was man's creation, invention, or discovery, but then again, it's not! I would have completely embraced this school of thought if I could affirm without a doubt that the world believed in marriage. But here again, I cannot!

If we know that the ruler of this world is the evil one, and his sole purpose in our lives is to steal, kill and destroy everything God has placed in our hands, in our minds and in our hearts, how then can we believe that he will give us the tools to have a successful marriage? What makes you believe that his intention is to preserve the sanctity of marriage? Can we be naïve enough to embrace and follow his advice? Can the most arrogant and selfish being ever be able to let go of his ego and love someone else unconditionally? Satan's goal is to break the covenant you and I have with our Maker, therefore, cause division among us. He does not know love, he obeys no rules, and submits to no one! Isn't that the attitude he wants us to adopt in our relationship; that self-seeking, self-centeredness and self-absorption? These are the total opposite of God's love. Let me ask you this; whose definition of love are you exemplifying? Whose principles are you applying, hoping to receive the promises and blessings God has promised to give His children?

Love is not self-seeking

Husbands are called to love their wives, and wives are instructed to submit to their husbands. It's not an accident that God made the focus on the spouse, and not on ourselves. Through the marriage covenant, each spouse loses authority over their own body. "*The wife does not have authority over her own body but yields it to her husband. In the same way, the husband does not have authority over his own body but yields it to his wife.*"

(1 Corinthians 7:4). They both share the responsibility to care, protect and provide. Since we were created with different wants and needs, we also will meet this responsibility in different ways. The most important need a man can have is to feel respected. I have noticed something first with my father and now with my husband, every time he comes home from work, he has the expectation that everyone will stop what they were doing to greet him and acknowledge his presence. It may seem insignificant, but I believe it tells us something about men; they need to be acknowledged, recognized a praised. They may not care much about flowers, nonetheless they like the attention, they like to feel admired and appreciated. Don't we often say, "men like to feel like kings"? but why is it that today, women no longer want to be queens or act like it? They want to wear the bigger crown. Let me stop here before I step ahead of myself. Anytime we deprive men of their most vital needs, we are consequently depriving ourselves of our raison d'être, our most important reason of being. We were made to be their help, to assist them in their mission to fill and subdue the earth. We were never created to subdue men, contrary to the popular beliefs. We will not be able to fulfill our purpose if we cannot submit. Submission is nothing other than to give men the respect and acknowledge the authority God has given them first.   Women were made to be loved, this is our most important need. We want to feel appreciated, cared for and desired. Men are made to protect and defend their wives and every fiber in their being seeks to do just that. But why are we witnessing more and more men failing to protect, provide and defend their spouse?   Women who fail to nurture, honor and respect their husbands? Have we not realized that we are part of one body, and whenever we don't fulfill

these responsibilities, aren't we sinking our own ships? Whatever we don't invest; we will never receive, whatever we refuse to sow; we will not reap! Can a house divided against itself stand? If you think that your spouse is not worth of the sacrifice you are making, compromise or adjustment, you will not be found worthy to inherit the blessings of the one who made them in His image.

Jesus calls the Church His bride, but today in the Church we are also witnessing preachers, shepherds taking advantage of their congregation, only finding motivation in their personal gains. What's in it for them? What can they do or say that will produce more offerings? They no longer care about the salvation, or the spiritual growth of the sheep, instead they are looking for innovative ways to deceive and cheat, to steal and oppress. The same way marriage has become transactional, the same way the Church is conducting business on the back of the people. Pastors are more concerned about their private jets, luxury cars or expensive houses rather than investing their time, pouring out the love of Christ that can heal and save the people and sharing the truth of the word of God. Can we manipulate God's word to our own benefit? How long do we think our God will remain silent?

Believers do the same. They go to church, participate in the activities that only benefit them. They don't mind spending hours at church, in prayer retreats or events as long as they get what they want. In the last decade, Churches have been filled with men and women looking for a spouse, a job or to meet other needs. And as soon as these needs are met, they can no longer find the time or the strength to attend. It's easy to blame the Pastor because he didn't call on birthdays, or when we lost a loved one. It's easy to pinpoint the flaws of our fellow brothers and sisters and to justify our lack of commitment and faith. Can we reach a point where we all acknowledge our weaknesses and shortcomings? Can we face the hard truth about our lack of responsibility and accountability? Can today be the day when we choose to look in the mirror and face the truth? Can we all admit that we were not completely sold out to Christ? Despite our "good" intentions, we resorted to our sinful nature, self-centered and self-driven motives. Everybody was in it with the hope of getting a return on their investment; except that the investment, was never actually made. We keep drawing from a well we never built, until we find another well, deeper than the first one. We can't keep complaining about the things we are not willing to change. We cannot expect from others a behavior we are not willing to demonstrate ourselves. We cannot ask for the Lord to bless us when we continually refuse to obey and trust Him. We cannot ask our spouse to love us when our definition of love places us at the center.

Love does not envy

We often hear "your spouse is not your enemy", but why do we even feel the need to restate this fact? The recent relationship between men and women seems to have taken an awful turn and more than ever, the competition has heightened on both sides because they see each other as adversaries, rather than partners. Men continue to silence or oppress women and make them feel invisible or disposable while women want to emasculate men and take the leadership; they are adamant about creating a future with little to no male presence. We must ask ourselves this question: what was the Lord's intent when he made them both male and female? Were they created to be in competition? The answer is obvious. They both are indispensable, with a common purpose, but very different ways to achieve. It has never been the Creator's design to see us engaging in this fierce yet subtle fight, that is now taking place.

Husbands and wives have lost their way of communication. They look at each other instead of having their eyes fixated on the Master. They can no longer see value in themselves that they start blaming one another. Have you lost your way with your Heavenly Father? Insecurity will cause men and women to become jealous and envious of each other. They will no longer celebrate each other but will perceive one's success as an individual accomplishment or evidence of their own failures, or will begin to criticize where called to encourage. They will choose to humiliate instead of appreciating and will destroy what was meant to be built. I can't help but wonder, whose traits we are demonstrating with such behaviors? "You belong to your father, the devil, and you want to carry out your father's desires" (John 8:44). Is this really what our God had in mind? Is this the way He intended for us to live together?

Though it's very sad to say, we must admit that we all have no appreciation for the precious gift God has given us in the person of our spouse. We either don't perceive their value or we choose not to, every time we can't see our own. And we give little or no time, attention or honor. We trample on them to the ground the same way we acted with our Savior Jesus, because we did not grasp or recognize His worth. What's your spouse worth? Do you treat her like an extension of yourself? Do you treat him with disdain and condescendence? Are you friends or enemies? Are you partners or adversaries? Do you love, respect, encourage and trust each other the way you were instructed to? Nobody should feel superior or inferior. God made us different to accomplish the same task, and to also reflect His fullness. Our differences are not a testament of anyone's weakness, but a testimony of God's glorious power, grace and wisdom. You are not your spouse's competition. Give God the glory by honoring, respecting and cherishing the person He has placed in your life.

Love does not dishonor

Do you remember the vows you pronounced on the day you decided to join your lives together? "I take you to be my wedded husband/wife. To have and to hold, from this day forward, for better, for worse, for richer, for poorer, in sickness and in health, to love and to cherish, till death do us part. And hereto I pledge you my faithfulness." Have you been living up to it? Are you doing everything in your power to fulfill this promise? What is preventing you from staying committed to the marriage? Have you lost your wonder? Have you failed in your mission to honor and respect, to protect and defend and to nurture and provide?

Love does not come from men, but God alone. He is the one who can fill our hearts with abundant love. Anytime we find ourselves away from His presence and out of His will, or doing things which do not glorify His Holy name; we are causing separation between He and us and subsequently with our spouse, making it almost impossible to love them.

> "Surely the arm of the Lord is not too short to save,
> nor his ear too dull to hear.
> But your iniquities have separated
> you from your God;
> your sins have hidden his face from you,
> so that he will not hear.

> For your hands are stained with blood,
> your fingers with guilt.
> Your lips have spoken falsely,
> and your tongue mutters wicked things."[30]

Our words, our actions drive a wedge between us and our Maker. Anytime we shame our spouse, disrespect them in public or in private, abuse them physically or verbally, anytime we fail to create an environment, conducive to the Holy Spirit to work within us; we take away from the meaning of our vows. We reduce our marriage to a living arrangement, not a covenant. We open a door to the enemy to step in and cause more chaos and confusion; driving us to sin and rebellion. How are you dishonoring your marriage vows? Have you told lies that are now starting to catch up with you? Whatever situation you may find yourself in, you always have an opportunity to come back and do something different. Remember His hand is not too short to save., but it all starts with the truth and a change of heart. Love rejoices with the truth[31].

Love is not proud

"Pride goes before destruction, and a haughty spirit before a fall" (Proverbs 16:18). How many marriages have been destroyed because of pride and unforgiveness? Marriage is not an arrangement in which each party seeks to benefit themselves. We are called to love each other as we love ourselves. Selfless love that pushes us to make sacrifice and compromises just to see the other person bloom and reach the purpose God has set for them. Every time we approach the relationship like a duel, there can be no winner. We both must seek to lay

---

[30] Isaiah 59:1-3
[31] 1 Corinthians 13

down our life, our agenda, our methods and principles and allow the Holy Spirit to mold us, shape us into the new entity He calls us to be. There is no "I" in team, if your spouse loses, you also lose. You may not find any reason to forgive or love again after you've been betrayed, mistreated or dismissed, but God's love covers a multitude of sins. Ask the Father for the strength to stand the course and reach the end goal; to be close to the Father. If light and darkness cannot coexist, the same is true for love and pride. Pride is the way of evil and not God, because it keeps the **focus on self, while love is geared towards others. Ask the Lord to soften your heart and show you the way, for without God; there is no love, no marriage.**

8
SEX TRAPS

In the beginning, man and woman were both naked and felt no shame. I used this reference, earlier, to highlight the need for every couple to walk in the truth, in complete honesty and transparency, being open to each other, without carrying the weight of shame. However, there is another dimension that needs to be addressed, as well; Intimacy.

Adam and Eve's nakedness was obviously physical. God intended for them to enjoy the gift of sex, find pleasure in each other's arms; learn how to join their bodies together and become one. They certainly did not feel embarrassed to show their birth mark, excess skin, or less flattering body parts. Nothing seems to be able to tarnish the joy they must have felt to be in each other's presence without feeling judged, scrutinized or compared to others. Can we say the same today for husband and wife? Can you get naked in front of your spouse and feel unashamed? Do you still believe in intimacy between you and your spouse? What lies of the enemy have you accepted to believe? Do you consider sex as gift or a curse, a servant or a master?

Immediately after Eve and Adam ate the fruit, they felt shame. They could no longer stand naked in the presence of the Lord, not without the fig leaves covering they made for themselves. It was the end of the intimacy they shared with their Maker and the beginning of human dissatisfaction. Suddenly, God's covering, His love and protection were not enough. They had opened the door for insecurity, embarrassment and shame to enter. Have you allowed the enemy to cripple your love life with shame and insecurity?

Shame in the bedroom

It's very important that we let go of the misconceptions, the myths we created around the physical intimacy between men and women. We must become aware of the evil tactics the enemy uses to ensnare us and destroy our marriages. Many couples shy away from the subject; it has been given either too little importance, thus, becoming a taboo, or given way too much attention, making it a commodity. For some, sex is only perceived as a means to an end or the end of everything. How many people got married only to obtain the freedom to sleep with their partner? How many got married only to realize they had absolutely nothing in common, except the bed they shared together? Some still have this grim on their face every time they hear or talk about sex and intimacy. They find little or no pleasure. Sex seems more like a punishment rather than a wonderful moment when two people fuse together and express their deepest love for one another. Could it be because love and marriage are no longer the requirement to have sex? Could it be because of the bestial images many have seen on TV, the sexual abuse many have experienced, associating intimacy with pain or perversion?
There seems to be such a profound disconnect between men and women. Nobody really wants to be vulnerable. The painful memories of the past and the inability to express needs or desires make it more difficult for them to experience pure joy, deep and intense pleasure that intimacy can bring. In many cases, it may be much easier to engage in sexual

intercourse without getting "attached", without any "pressure" to commit, without having to be exposed, living this fallacy that sex can be independent from everything else. We believe sex does not, and should not involve our feelings and emotions. Basically, we can give our bodies without ever giving our hearts. Isn't this what happening with our worship? We are physically present; speaking, singing and praising with our lips while our hearts remain out of touch. We can be in Church, take part in every activity without ever giving our hearts to the Lord, without ever allowing His personal touch, His Holy Spirit to drop a seed inside of us. We deny ourselves the opportunity to experience real transformation that comes from a time spent with our Maker in real intimacy.

We need to realize that physical intimacy was never supposed to occur outside the covenant of marriage; it was never intended to be used as a form of payment, a manipulation tool or a way to exert power.

Trophy wives, sex slaves

Children, especially girls are ignorant of their bodies. Many grow up feeling ashamed of their sexual desires. Often taught to suppress their needs or feelings, they become adult and can't seem to reconcile the idea that if God created sex, then it is a good thing. They cannot embrace the reality that sex between husband and wife is the ultimate expression of love and symbolizes a desire to become one. It may very well be impossible to have a different perception when the only time they discovered their sexuality was through rape, molestation or abuse. How can they see value, appreciate when they were robbed of the chance to choose? They were never taught about the concept, and this cycle must be broken! Both girls and boys must be taught about the gift of sex in the context of marriage, and should also be informed about the ways the enemy can use this to bring perversion, confusion and pain. "*Do not arouse or awaken love until it so desires."(Song of Solomon 8:4).*

We may not even think that in our Christian world, women are being treated like slaves or are being abused by their own husbands. How many stories have we heard? Even in this new era where women claim to be emancipated and independent, many are still being used as sex toys. In the eyes of many, sex still represents a means to an end. The only time and place they seem to have some value, is at night; in the bedroom. Some husbands have used the commandment of submission to dominate and overpower their wives. Although we recognize that many women still feel powerless, undervalued, misunderstood, abused and defeated, we must admit that some have also used their physical attributes to seduce and lure men. Whatever the situation may be, sex is not and should not be used as a power switch.

Hidden gem

Too many men and women suffer in silence. Too many have heard and believed the lies of the enemy. And they have either built their marriage around their bedroom skills or have learned to live without it. There is a disproportionate amount of information one can find in connection with intimacy. The world gives a plethora of "ideas" about love, marriage and sex while the Church offers almost nothing, except for the bans and the limitations. In the eyes of many, sex is a terrible thing, repugnant and distasteful. Or, in very few instances, it would be described as the most boring thing married couples could ever do together and

cursed be those who find any pleasure in it.
We have the responsibility to restore the truth or else we will fail as parents, as leaders as disciples of Christ. We may be silent if we want but silence will never make things better or disappear. Today, too many couples get engaged with unrealistic expectations. They have no prior understanding of the nature of the covenant they seek to enter, they have a distorted perception even when it comes to their marital obligations. Too many assumptions are being made on the subject. What would it take for all of us to have open Christ centered conversations on sex and relationship? Have we bought into the lie of the enemy and changed God's view on intimacy between husband and wife? Or should we go back to Song of Solomon's fiery love declarations, sexual hints?
Sex is a gift from God to married people and it must be perceived as such. If we continue to live in guilt and shame, if we choose to hide and tiptoe around it, we will give ground to the enemy to instill more lies and deceive many more.
Husbands and wives must understand and appreciate the infinite gift we have in sexual intimacy. We must find the courage to be open and express our needs and desires, without feeling ashamed, embarrassed or too "worldly" because sex does not come from the world, it comes from our heavenly Father. There is nothing wrong in finding pleasure in the arms of your spouse. Let the truth of the word of God destroy the walls and break the silence.
We often highlight the importance of good communication between partners, but this also applies to intimacy. Husbands and wives must both feel comfortable to trust each other enough to freely express their needs. Can two walk together unless they agree? Will you be able to bloom in your sexual

relationship with your spouse unless you both agree on what should be done and how? When it comes to sex and intimacy, we must remain within the boundaries established by our Creator. Whatever you do, it must be in agreement with your spouse, but most importantly in concordance with the word of God. There are many speculations about what's permissible and what's not. I cannot pretend to have all the answers, but I believe the Holy Spirit is the one who convinces us of sin, righteousness and judgment. Whatever we do, we must ask the Lord, and be sensitive to the needs and the physical or emotional limitations of our partner.

More than One

When marriage resembles more a contract than a covenant, it becomes relatively easy to seek after our personal gain. Individual satisfaction trumps the couple's growth and needs. We become more obsessed with our own happiness, forsaking the very nature of the vows we pronounced on the day of the wedding. We would withdraw, give up and walk away for any or no reason. Can you imagine our God, our bridegroom walking away from us every time we walk in sin and disobedience? Every time we turn away from Him, and place everyone or everything else on the throne of our hearts? Though we fall short of God's glory each day, His mercy and lovingkindness always make a way for us.

Marriage, in the eyes of the Lord is everlasting, selfless, enduring, forgiving, trusting. It requires dedication and commitment, doing everything to stand strong together. It leaves no doors open, has no alternate plan. Two people who never stop choosing each other despite the obstacles, challenges and difficulties. They place their faith, not in themselves or in each other but in the Almighty God, the One who was at the beginning of the relationship, who is in their midst and will be forever. It's about togetherness, being one with the Holy Spirit, totally depending on Him to shape us, mold us, and lead us through the storms of life. Instead, we have become unfaithful in our words, thoughts or actions. We've allowed our spouse's behavior or weaknesses to dictate our decisions, our obligations, our feelings. We reassess God's commandment to love and respect our spouse every day, depending on "their" righteousness.

More than ever we witness couples redefining the Lord's instruction.

Women will submit if and when the men will show love and appreciation or vice versa. We make concessions or sacrifice, only in the light of our own interests. We have learned to accommodate the needs of our partner, giving them room to lie, cheat and deceive. Infidelity, adultery is the new normal. Whether this is considered as an upgrade or an optional feature, it surely has found a way to become part of the "marriage deal". What's more horrifying is how easy it has been to convince women to accept the fact. Today, many believe that the only way to make marriage work is to accept infidelity, marital indiscretions. They remain helpless and powerless or, the brave ones in the midst will follow the lead and find a lover themselves. They somehow assume they will have the upper hand by becoming the villain, too; their pain, humiliation will be lessened, and the lesson will be taught. Whatever the rationale is, the result could not be more outrageous. Everything is permissible as long as we stay married, right? For the Lord, our God hates divorce. Is divorce the only thing the Lord hates?

Broken vows

Didn't the Lord make you one with your wife?[32] Why then are we faithless to each other?[33] How did that happen? Where did we get the idea that adultery was acceptable or not reprehensible? What made us believe for one second that men or women could have multiple partners, or have extra marital affairs without repercussions? Why have we, women accepted infidelity as an inextricable part of marriage? Did we take the Lord's mercy for granted or did we rely on the encounter between Jesus and the adulterous woman to assume that it wasn't so terrible after all? Did we get to thinking that adultery is only punishable when it comes from a woman?

The world earnestly tries to convince us that men's instinct is to cheat. They cannot and should not even be expected to remain faithful to their spouse. Since when were we created to follow our instincts? We are spiritual beings, called to be led by the Holy Spirit, and not follow our senses, emotions or intelligence. Should we really believe that men are predestined to be adulterous because of some hormones or natural predispositions? Do women not have eyes that see beautiful things? Do they not have physical needs and sexual desires, too? Can they never feel temptation? Why should women refrain from cheating on their husbands, while men get a pass? If women believe infidelity is wrong, sexual immorality is a sin. Why is it that we have condoned the unfaithfulness of our fathers, husbands and sons?

I told you in the introduction (now I see why He made me share these details) how I went this past summer to my hometown of Abidjan and the Lord gave me so

---

[32] Malachi 2:15 NLT
[33] Malachi 2:10 ESV

many words about the country's adulterous behavior, the sexual immorality of the people. In a few words, I will try to share the not so pleasant conversation we had. "You have accepted what I've rejected. You excuse what I accuse." There was no confusion as to where the Lord stands on the question of unfaithfulness. "*Let marriage be honorable among all, and let the marriage bed be without defilement, for God will judge sexually immoral people and adulterers." (Hebrews 13:4)*. How many times did the Lord punish or vow to destroy Israel and Judah because of their unfaithfulness? Do we not think that God, who created both men and women, know us better than anyone else? Could he not know that unfaithfulness was at the core of man? Why would He punish something that himself designed? Should he then expect us to be faithful when adultery and prostitution was woven into our innermost being?

God will never condone or bless an adulterous relationship. Women should not either. We cannot accept because we don't know what to do or we don't want to "lose" our marriage. If we understand how sacred the covenant of marriage is, we will change our approach. Men and women have no power, without the Holy Spirit. Our Father in Heaven never anticipates for us to live life in our own strength. In Jesus we become new creation. If He resisted temptation, it was because of the Lord's power at work. He did nothing outside of the will and the limitations His father had set. We are called to walk in the same light. Submit to the Lord, resist the devil and it will flee.

Adulterers don't just break the vows they made to their spouse, they also dishonor and break the covenant they have with the Lord. Women need to understand that they have a responsibility unto the Lord, as well. He will hold us accountable, not for the mistakes of our spouse but for our response to their infidelity. Are we creating an atmosphere that fosters immorality, wickedness and debauchery or are we upholding God's standards and morals? What if women learned how to rely more on the Lord, seeking to please Him, instead of men? Could it be that women do not believe God is powerful enough to protect and defend their marriage against the destructive sin of adultery? Have we allowed our hearts to be filled with pride, and begin to think our will must be God's will? How often do we decide to stay in a marriage that we know should have never occurred? How many times have we lied or convinced ourselves that what we want was inspired by the Lord? The enemy has celebrated way too many parties in too many lives. He wants us to doubt God's power while we lean more on our strengths. Marriage is not between men alone; it begins and ends with God. Unless the Lord builds the house, adultery, sin, confusion, chaos will have a room.

Bearing fruits

You may expect me to talk about pornography, masturbation, fornication, all these sex traps that destroy countless marriages and lives, however, I will not. Not because they are irrelevant, but they are inherently connected to everything we've previously addressed. However, we will end this chapter with the unexpected, this almost odd topic that leaves everyone on edge. You may have guessed it already; abortion! A small word, or often a quick decision which nevertheless carries so much weight, and whose consequences have been disastrous. Why should we talk about it, since it's a "personal" choice, which affects no one except the person who chooses to undergo the "procedure"? Why then, do we have two ideologies so diametrically opposed? Pro-life versus pro-choice.

One group seeks to uphold the sanctity of life and seeks to protect the rights of the unborn child, while the other group gives preeminence to the mother who must be able to make her own decisions regarding her reproductive system. They claim that a woman should not be forced to carry a pregnancy, against her will. There is another group, almost never acknowledged (because we don't really think they affect the outcome) but this group believes in finding the balance between the two. They may not encourage abortion but will not necessarily condemn those who want to commit it. They may feel torn between the two and want to reconcile both sides. Is this possible? Can we protect the life of the unborn child and respect the choice of the mother, at the same time? Well, the answer may seem obvious, but it wasn't so for me up until recently. On the issue of abortion, I have been one of the people Jesus would call "lukewarm". I never stood for abortion, never considered it as an option, but I never firmly stood against it. I was, or thought I was, being considerate, sensitive to others' opinions and perceptions, and I never really gave a second thought to my "position".

In more recent years, my prayer has been inspired by Psalm 37:4 *"Take delight in the LORD, and he will give you the desires of your heart."* I never imagined this will lead me to become more radical in some ways than I may have even wished. When Jesus calls us to follow him, He doesn't take us where *we* want to go, He takes us where *He* needs us to be. I had also been forced to admit that my thoughts had little or no incidence on God's plan. He cannot be swayed or changed, His Word does not evolve to align with our culture, our desires or even our "needs". God is the same yesterday, today and forever. What He hated yesterday will not change today because we live in a "post Christian" world. "*Heaven and earth will pass away, but my words will never pass away[34]*".

About three months ago, I had this dream. It seemed like I was on an airplane and someone was sitting next to me. I got up and went to what looked like a hallway, and it also looked like I was standing in front of a long line of metal tables; a bit like in a chain factory. There were babies, lots of tiny babies, with their legs and joints broken. I could actually see someone breaking their body parts. Others were in clear plastic bags, going down the chain one after the other. They made no sound. I heard no noise, no cry, no sound at all. I remember looking dismayed, in total shock. I looked at one baby in particular; she was in a clear plastic bag, she stared at me but made no sound, neither a blink, nor a cry, almost static. I can still remember the look on her face; it gives me chills just to think about it. I remember screaming, yelling, asking the people to stop. I asked, "why are you doing this?" and I wanted them to stop but nobody was listening; they did not care and they did not stop either. I think they could not even see or hear me so I began to scream louder, weeping and wailing. I felt so helpless, I went back to my seat and the dream ended. As I woke up, I was completely shaken and very intrigued. I was trying to understand the meaning of the dream. So, I prayed and asked the Lord. He simply replied: "Abortion. That's what it is. That's exactly what they do to these babies. These babies are alive. See, you pray and lament over your children being killed. These poor kids, you say, they deserve to live. Why killing innocent lives? But you remain silent over the babies being killed in the womb." I didn't need more explanation, I didn't need a move of

---
[34] Matthew 24:35

the Holy Spirit to make me understand how my position, or lack thereof concerning abortion was not in alignment with God's heart desire. He wants us to receive His seed and bear fruits in His image, and this is another reason why we should preserve our bodies (God's temple) until marriage. Otherwise, we will form soul ties that will compromise the beautiful and Holy seeds God wants to plant inside of us.

Again, about a week ago, I was at our church prayer breakfast and the Lord dropped in my heart to pray for various segments of the population. As soon as I started to pray for our armed officers, my heart broke and I started to weep as I was feeling pain in my womb. I was crying and mourning for the mothers who lost their children due to police brutality, but also the mothers of these soldiers who work every day to keep us safe. They too have lost their children. and the Lord said "this is how I feel for every one of my children who dies. How many children have I lost? "We may not feel the need to pick a side, but God wants us to love what He loves and hate what He hates. He is calling us to stand to protect and uphold the value and dignity of life as tall as we stand to defend the sanctity of marriage. Abortion comes as a thief to steal, kill and destroy the seed that God plants within us. It robs us of the promises and the blessings of our bridegroom. "The sin of abortion comes with a spirit of rejection over many families" says the Lord.

9
OUT OF ORDER

One of the biggest issues Christians face today is submission. It's not just about the wives not submitting to their husbands; it's the body of Christ who is acting with a total disregard for the Word of God. We, as the bride of Christ are called to submit to the power and the will of our Bridegroom, the Almighty King, however, there seems to be a spirit of rebellion trying to control the people. Hearts are being hardened, eyes refuse to see, ears refuse to hear and though our mouths are opened, they speak lies and reject the truth.

We live in this world of false pretenses, trying to "maintain appearances", trying to "control the optics". What was considered wrong is now right and what was right, has now become wrong. The truth matters not, anymore. Do you know the adage; *beauty is in the eye of the beholder*? Well, today, truth is in the ear of the listener. Truth is a relative thing these days and it has become people's possession; my truth, your truth, his truth, their truth, only because we have rejected The Truth; Jesus is the way, the truth and the life[35]. However, today we don't want to take the narrow road that leads to Him, we want to create as many roads as possible, and make our own way to Him. It's no longer what Jesus said, its more about how you hear it, how you feel about it and how you see it. The

---
[35] John 14:6

same scripture means something when I talk to my sister, but the complete opposite if it relates to someone I don't particularly like.

My vision, your vision

On the day of Pentecost, all the Apostles were together in one place. They did not each stand on their way or in their truth; they were in one accord and the Spirit of the Lord moved. Today, we are shutting the door to the Holy Spirit because of division, disunity and disagreement. We always see what the other person is saying as opposed to what we say. Did it ever occur to you that what they are saying could also be supporting what you're thinking or trying to convey? How many times has this happened in a conversation? Take a couple, the husband may say something, and the wife hears it out of one ear, she totally gets it wrong and start arguing; then everyone around will now try to explain the "misunderstanding". Later on, everyone will finally realize they were both saying the same thing.

Too often, husbands and wives have a contentious relationship because they fail to realize that they are both players on the same team; they can hardly trust each other because their visions seem not to align. Remember the Tower of Babel? The people not only were defying the Lord Almighty, they were also trying to create new ways to reach God, to be God, and it led to division, confusion and chaos. The same thing is happening today. We may not try to build a tower per se, but we are finding multiple avenues to reach God. We define God based on our abilities and our capacities to "hold" Him. It's all about the size of our cup! Nonetheless, God is not a man to be controlled, neither is He a thing to be contained or possessed. He is God, all by Himself, and your opinion of Him will never affect who He is. However, our opinion of God will affect who *we* are, and the things *we* do.

When God created man and woman and joined them in the sacred covenant of marriage, He gave them one vision, one mission. For the vision to come alive, they must leave everything else, forsake all others and become One. Agreement, unity is what activates the Holy Spirit. He doesn't move where there is division. But look what is being created now.

The enemy cannot destroy the vision God gave you, just like he could not take back God's words to Adam, instead he goes to your spouse and drop these little nuggets, we call them "ideas" or "thoughts" and convinces them that things will be so much easier, more convenient if they stepped up and did something different. I am not implying that different is bad, but when different is working 'against' and not 'for', it becomes a problem. As I stated earlier, God made women different than men; we are simply wired differently, but we have the same mission. So, our differences help facilitate the accomplishment of the goal, but the enemy of our souls is working to prevent God's purpose to come to pass in our lives. Therefore, he uses these new ideas, new truths to bring confusion and division. Did you think this new idea was going to work, but you now realize that you and your spouse are walking in separation and not in agreement? Convenience will destroy your purpose and comfort will abort your mission. Do you think Jesus was comfortable on the cross of Calvary?

For God's vision to manifest in your life, you must accept to go through the fire. It will be painful, difficult, uncomfortable and inconvenient, but through the fire you will be refined, reshaped, molded and softened to make you one with your spouse. God cannot bring you together if you refuse to go under. There is no togetherness without submission. We need to realize that both husband and wife are not called to devise their own plans. It's not about who has the best idea, the best plan, the best vision; t's not a you versus me thing; it is you *and* me. Together we must submit to the Lord's plan and His vision. He is not trying to get us to agree with what our spouse is saying, He is calling us to know Him, discern His will for us and to obey. There can be no division, no confusion when we both follow Christ. Submission is not unto a man, it is to the authority and the leadership of Christ, therefore, men must seek the Lord for themselves, and not rely on their wives to "pray" them in. Wives must also learn how to trust and obey God and they will be able to submit and respect their husbands, who in turn will be submitted to the Lord.

Men with narrow shoulders

For this section I was thinking of "out of position" or "out of line" something like that and the Lord dropped these words in my spirit "men with narrow shoulders". I never really thought about anything like this before. Out of curiosity, I even looked online to see if there was an apparent problem with men with narrow shoulders (Oh, the things we read on the internet). It may seem like some find it very unattractive, because it gives the perception of weakness. Men are supposed to exude strength and power, so they will train long hours to build those muscles. Is this still the case today? Do we still expect men to have broad shoulders? We may not, but the Lord does and not the way we may think. It's not about the look, the physical appearance, as it is a matter of position.

For many years, I was almost convinced due to all the

things I was hearing, that position was a man thing and not a God thing. We made it seem like position was such a terrible thing. But I have long realized that our God is a God of order. We each have a place and a position in the Kingdom of God. We are the Sons and the Daughters of the Most High, heirs of God and co-heirs with Christ[36]. We do not seek a seat, a place or a title that was never given to us. We must be aware of who we are in the eyes of our Father if we want to have access to Him and claim what's rightfully ours. In that same way, we will recognize our prerogatives and our responsibilities. Too many Christians live in bondage because they have not yet grasped the reality of the Word; they walk crippled by fear, calling it humility. Knowing who you are, where you belong, who you serve, on whom you stand is not arrogance or pride. Pride leads us to covet what does not belong to us, but if God said, "this is yours, take it", who are we to say otherwise?

If the U.S. army has its generals, lieutenants and other official rankings and so forth, do you think God's army would not? Obviously, God's Kingdom is not like that of men, nevertheless, there is order, because order will bring about respect. As I said earlier, we do not seek position to rule over people or to boost our ego. God is the one who establishes rulers and kings. But we, each have a position in God's kingdom, a role to play, a specific task to accomplish and we can only do it with the Holy Spirit, not by our own strength, not by might, not by power, only by the spirit of the Lord.[37]

Our position in Christ is not a matter of superiority or inferiority, because we are all equal in God's eyes. One is not above the other, no one is better than the other. We just have different parts to play, thus different gifts

---

[36] Romans 8:17
[37] Zechariah 4:6

and abilities. We are the body remember? We all need each other and no one could and will replace another. God made each one of us unique and special. Men and women have their position in the Kingdom. Can we say men are the head? Could women be the hands? Would it matter if the head was all strong and powerful but had no hands to help execute the vision – the plan? Would it matter if the hands were super pretty, well-manicured, strong and polished but had no clue about what the plan was? And I am not reducing men or women to either one, but I want us to understand that everything God does has a purpose and nothing that the enemy is trying to depict should matter when we know who we are and what we are called to do.

Why did I say that it mattered to God that men have broad shoulders? Does he not look at the inward appearance rather than the external things? I wasn't referring to men's physical appearance, either, but wanted us to get a better picture of what God wants to achieve in the natural, as well. Since the beginning of times, God has placed the mantle of authority over the men. He has entrusted them with the mission to conquer, protect, defend and provide. He made them strong and powerful physically, with a deeper tone to their voice. He made them care about the great things, not the small. He made them strong enough to protect, but weak enough to need someone else. Men have relinquished their rights and shied away from their responsibilities. They have taken a back seat and let women redefine the rules. They have fallen into a slumber, and nothing seems to be able to awaken them. We have children in men's body, looking for mothers instead of wives. They either refuse to lead or simply cannot lead because they have not yet dealt with the pain and the hurt in their life. They are emotionally or intellectually unable to assess the situation and take charge. Others prefer the comfort of the back seat rather than facing the peril of the front-line battles. Comfort will abort your mission. Women have picked up a weight that was never intended for them to carry, because the men have walked out, away from God's presence. Husbands, you were never created to sit back but to walk ahead, defend, protect and love. Wives, you were not created to rule, or overpower, but to submit and help. If men cannot do it alone, what makes us think women could?

The future is female

With the rise of "feminism" and "independent" women, we have slowly but surely removed the jewels of our crowns, one piece at the time. It may not look like it, but this is what's happening. Are we not walking away from our primary roles? Did I just say roles? Is there such a thing as male or female roles? Are they not both capable of doing the same things, equally? Should we still try to differentiate the roles between men and women?
We are all aware of the paradigm shift, but are we still walking on the path that was created for us? Did our Omniscient, Omnipotent God make a mistake when He made us male and female? Do gender differences not matter anymore? This is what feminism is about. It's not about female recognition or empowerment like some want to believe. Many fall in the trap because they feel like their voices are being heard, and they now have a platform and a "power" that they never thought they would have. Strong, powerful women have now taken the scene and are making decisions, and everyone must watch out! They need no man to tell them what to do, how or when. They are strong by themselves. They are their own kind of beautiful, their

own kind of powerful. They can be mothers without being glued to any man, they can decide what they want to do with their own bodies, they are the epitome of independence. They are bold, confident, and can change the world. This would have been true only if it was not lacking a vital component. Not any single person, male or female was ever able to conceive a child without the other. Men and women have more differences than the clothes they wear or the way they look. We have physiological and psychological differences that make us unique and inimitable. Men and women are not interchangeable. Though the goal of feminism is to blur the line, to erase the fundamental differences between male and female, we, as Christians cannot adopt any views that are antithetic to the Word of God. The purpose of feminism is not to empower women, but to take them out of position, to lead them in a direction that God never intended for them. Feminism is nothing else but a modern way to enslave and ostracize women, by giving them a false sense of control and security – a new wave of rebellion. Women are not fighting against men to "reclaim" their power or have a seat at the table. They are rejecting the very essence of womanhood.

Women were never created to be independent. God formed Eve out of a man's rib so she could remain protected, covered. Jesus calls us to become His disciples, His followers. We are His bride. Is this a coincidence or a mistake that the most important thing our Lord did for us was to give his Son to show us His love? Women need to be loved, and our bridegroom showed us just that. He is the Vine and we are the branches; apart from Him, we can't do anything. Will this also be a coincidence that *He* made female out of man to establish an interdependence? Is this not one of the most basic needs women have? To feel loved and protected? Nevertheless, women have left their place on the battlefield to chase after the illusion of power and control. I read this quote by Timothy Leary, an American psychologist and writer *"Women who seek to be equal with men lack ambition."* I don't think this is a mere lack of ambition, but a profound lack of understanding, wisdom and knowledge and without knowledge, God's people will perish. The enemy is not concerned about women wearing slacks or men wearing dresses and makeup, he is after our identity, our position, and most importantly, our seed. If he can make us step out of place, he will be able to destroy the most important thing: our relationship with Christ.

The dragon is after your seed (Revelation 12). Wouldn't it be easier if he could just prevent you from carrying any seed instead of having to wait around to devour your child? There is such a great spirit of rebellion in America and around the world today. Children are turning against their parents, husbands against wives, brothers against sisters. Church goers are many, but they carry no seed, there is no transformation. We are either in a deep sleep like Adam was, too apathetic to do a thing or like Martha, too busy to sit still, listen and learn. Now that the world praises independent women, they want more superwomen who think they can do it all. Pride is rooted deeper in us than we are willing to admit. Women are starting to believe they can create a new world that will be better than the one God made. We have lost appreciation for the treasures He has placed inside of us. Women no longer want to be vulnerable, warm, wise, gentle and kind. In their mind, being submissive is synonym with inferiority, worthlessness or being invisible. So, they make these superhero capes and take on a mission that was never assigned to them, carrying a weight way too heavy for their narrow shoulders. Why does this sound familiar?

Was this the objective – to reverse the roles and create chaos? We have somehow confused independence with autonomy. The same way women believe they can do it all, without the men, we as God's children have also started to believe we can do everything without Him. We've placed more confidence in ourselves, our successes, performances and abilities. We erect, every day, new altars for the idols on the throne of our hearts, whether it's our ambition, our social media, our fears or our insecurities. Have we been set free to fall into a new form of oppression or bondage? Why are God's people living in profound disregard for God's will?

Confusion, Chaos & Conflict

I cannot say this without feeling the hair on the back of my neck stand up. Our God has a fight to pick with His sons and His daughters. For both have failed to uphold the sanctity of the covenant we have with Him.

"He will cover you with his feathers, and under his wings you will find refuge; his faithfulness will be your shield and rampart[38]."

Men have failed in their duty to love their wives like Christ loved the Church and remained faithful to her. They need understand how they are to exemplify the faithfulness of God and be a representation of Him in the eyes of their wives. Husbands are called to cover their wives like Christ covers us with his wings. This is why I mentioned earlier that it's no coincidence that God made Eve out of Adam's rib – to create a shelter, and edge of protection around her, to keep her close to his heart and allow her to feel the warmth of his love.

---

[38] Psalm 91:4

But countless times, we've witnessed husbands who lack honesty, transparency and even accountability. Men have abused their prerogatives and have tried to control, oppress, deny or suppress women's rights and silence their voices. Due to the incredible high number of physical, emotional abuse that women have suffered, and continue to suffer every day, we may be able to understand why the "independent women" movement seems so attractive. It feels like an answer to their prayer, the cry of their hearts. It may seem like they ae finally getting a chance to be seen and be heard. They believe it's their opportunity to take back what was stolen from them – their dignity, honor, self-esteem, and way too often their ability to make a choice. Although I understand how feminism may seem like the best way to revendicate and reclaim what was stolen, I think it goes against the very thing God is asking us to do: submit and trust. Believe and obey. Yes, we are to denounce, condemn and reject violence, rape, abuse or other form of oppression, but it must never be done with contempt to the Word of God.

Men may be either too controlling or too apathetic, but they are called to be the head and lead. We must understand how the enemy has used sexual abuse, molestation, and the likes to instill doubt, fear, hurt and pain in our hearts. How can we trust and submit to the ones who hurt us so deeply? When a father, uncle, cousin or friend, meant to love and protect us, but instead, robs us of our innocence, our dignity, how are we to trust again? Every time husbands are unfaithful to their wives, they enlarge the gap and push them away and out of God's presence.

Men may have hurt, betrayed, abandoned, despised you, but rebellion will never heal your pain. Only God can. The enemy wants you to doubt God's love and faithfulness based on your husband's actions or lack thereof.

Women are not without blame either. We've failed to take our place by believing the lies of the enemy and letting our hearts be filed with shame, pain and unforgiveness. We are called to honor our spouses, to nurture the precious gifts God has placed inside of them. Yes, they too, have incredible and unique talents to perform the duties assigned to them. But women have failed to pray for their men, husbands, sons or fathers – encourage and seek ways to help them in their God ordained mission. Instead, we have come up with "new ideas," "new ways" to make it happen, to protect ourselves, to become "independent". We have been misled into thinking that if men cannot be trusted, then God also could not be trusted. If God allowed bad things to happen to us, then He must not really love us either. We have reached the conclusion that we could not or should not depend on men, anymore.

It is time that we allow the truth of the Word of God to penetrate our minds, our hearts and transform our perspective. His faithfulness endures forever and is certainly not conditioned by men's.

Lord Jesus, come into our hearts, renew our minds, open our eyes and let us see the good things that you have set before us. I pray for our men, that you will wake them out of their slumber, and give them back the scepter. Help them walk in your truth, your light and your love. Teach them to lead without controlling. I also pray for us women that you would heal and mend our broken hearts. Teach us how to follow with poise, grit and wisdom, without blaming or criticizing. Let us wear the crown of glory that you have reserved for those who love and obey you. In Jesus name.

PART 4

RESTORING "ONENESS"

10
REALITY CHECK

"All of us like sheep have strayed away. We have left God's path to follow our own[39]." Most of the issues we face today are the byproduct of our disobedience and sin. We have chosen and continue to choose the wider paths which lead to destruction, forgetting our Lord. Marriages are in shambles, not because men and women are poor husbands and wives, but because we've become wayward children. We no longer abide and rest in the shadow of the Almighty. It's easier to follow the world's rules and principles, if any, than to submit to His will. *"Call to me and I will answer you and tell you great and unsearchable things you do not know."* (Jeremiah 33:3). There are many things that we, as humans, have no knowledge about, that we cannot even begin to understand; yet, we have a heavenly Father, who is eager to not only teach us everything we need to know, but to hold our hands and guide us through it all. If only we did not make room in our hearts for offense and pride, we would have more humility and wisdom to see the concealed things that the Holy Spirit yearns to reveal to us. What have you allowed your mind to be filled with? What's in your heart that is preventing you from loving and trusting the Lord your God?

It's very important to realize that our relationship with others cannot get any better, unless we release the

---

[39] Isaiah 53:6 NLT

destructive thoughts, the painful memories, the traumatic experiences, the labels or false accusations from our mind, soul and body; but we are not to do it alone.

The Bridegroom

I hope it would not be presumptuous to assume that the difference between wedding and marriage is well established. I also have no doubt that we pretty much have a clear understanding about living marriage as a covenant versus a contract, and that our expectations may even be more defined now. However, I am a little afraid that many may not have a good grasp on the identity of the person we are entering this covenant with. Who is He? What do we know about Him? Too often, we say yes to the ring without knowing the person. We want the relationship without the commitment. We want the diamond but run away from the fire. We want the title without the responsibilities. Do you know why God revealed himself under all these different names and attributes? So that we may know Him and believe in Him. For He is all the things He says He is, and He can do all the things He says He can do. As the bridegroom, Jesus loves us, he gave up his life for us to sanctify and make us whole. Can you believe that the love of Christ is enough to sustain you for the rest of your life? He is our redeemer, provider, protector, deliverer; our defender and our Hope. He is the Faithful One "*who will sustain you to the end, guiltless in the day of our Lord Jesus Christ.[40]*" Though we constantly choose to live in sin and disobedience, Jesus's love and faithfulness are not conditional or based upon our faithless behavior.

---

[40] 1 Corinthians 1:8 ESV

And though we are not worthy of the sacrifice he made for us, His hand is never too far that we cannot reach. But we must come to him, with a repentant heart, acknowledge our mistakes and he will forgive us. *"If we confess our sins, he is faithful and just and will forgive us our sins and purify us from all unrighteousness."* (1John 1:9)

The one who forgives

Marriage is a process, an adventure, a journey to become one. It does not happen overnight or by the touch of a magic wand. Two people with very different personalities, life experiences, backgrounds, values and perspectives must learn how to fuse them – blend them together to recreate a new canvas.

Even though this section is titled around forgiveness, I do not want to expand too much on it or give you this long sermon on why we should forgive each other. Instead, I want us to focus on grace and patience. Why? Because we cannot forgive unless we have an understanding. We may not agree, we may not condone the behavior, but patience will give us the courage to hope that things will get better. Hold tight, while I unpack this.

Again, we get married to people who may look, speak or act nothing like us, and in most cases, these differences are what attracted us to them. After a while, we realize that we are going in separate directions, doing things which may not always bring us closer together. So, what do we do? We become impatient, begin to feel helpless and weary. We start to question the very reasons why we decided to join our lives together. Suddenly, we can no longer see God's handprints all over like we used to, and we quickly assume it wasn't God after all. Let me say this, and I will be very blunt. If you did get married with the assurance that God was front and center of your relationship, and you can't see that anymore, well you may want to check your heart. You may need to assess your relationship with Him. Are you still hearing and listening to His voice or have you decided to follow a new route? Too often, we place the blame on our spouses and refuse to reflect on our own motives and behaviors. Why did I mention grace? Because none of us is perfect. We are sinners in our own ways, but God's love is so perfect that He never rejects nor condemns us. Can we also understand that marriage is to last for a lifetime, and our Maker knew exactly that some things may require that exact amount of time to be the way He had intended; but we don't have the patience to wait or the grace to forgive.

Today, I want to ask you to let the Lord search your heart and reveal to you every area of unforgiveness, narrow-mindedness, that the enemy may be using to destroy the plans of God for your marriage. I will also ask that you take the time to realign your views with God's will. It's never too late to come back and let the Lord take you in a new direction. If you are the one who needs to ask for forgiveness, do it without delay. Do not let your heart get hardened, any longer. Be humble, acknowledge the hurt, show remorse, let His light shine through.

The way, the truth and the life

We can all agree – there is no love without trust. Marriage cannot endure if we walk in darkness. Couples are required to be honest with each other – naked and unashamed, remember? Do you have trust issues in your marriage? What's stopping you from being open, honest and vulnerable?

Men, in general, like to believe they can do almost anything in their own strength. We think we will have an amazing life together with our spouse, and some of these crazy stories we hear about other people's marriages will never happen to us and we quickly realized what a myth it was – and it's not because we stopped wishing or believing, it's just that the reality is completely different. Why? Because men cannot work this thing called marriage alone. Marriage is from God, with God, and for God's glory. Unless the builder builds the house...we already know it is doomed to fail. We cannot have an honest relationship with anyone, even ourselves unless the truth lives in us. You want your husband or your wife to be more truthful, less secretive, start by inviting the God of all truths in your life, your heart, your home. For when Jesus, the light of the world, comes into our lives, darkness must flee, lies are exposed and healing can begin.

Too many married couples live as if they were roommates or single. What secret are you keeping from your spouse? What are you afraid or ashamed of? Don't let fear, guilt or shame hold you captive. I pray that the Almighty God will reveal and expose anything that is causing mistrust and embarrassment in your marriage. You and your spouse are called to become one in every aspect of life, not just physically. You cannot keep your emotions, your dreams and goals, your finances, your weaknesses and insecurities hidden in a secret place to which only you have the key. It's time to make room for the Holy Spirit. Morning has come, the light will shine.

God's choice or yours?

"I said, 'I will never break my covenant with you, and you shall not make a covenant with the people of this land, but

you shall break down their altars.' Yet you have disobeyed me." (Judges 2:1-2). There are many times in the bible where the people of God were told or forbidden to marry or make covenants with a certain group of people. We may not recognize the Ammonites or the Hittites in our society today. Does this mean we are free to marry whoever we choose to? Isn't this what we hear almost every day? *"You are free to marry whom you choose, nobody should tell you who to love..."*, except, a child of God, a son or a daughter of the Most High God is free indeed, but their freedom is to do the will of the Father[41]. We are called to love everyone, not to be in covenant with anyone. We may not read it explicitly, the same way it was in old testament times, but the Apostle Paul reminds us of this truth. Can light and darkness coexist?

Our purpose on this earth is to accomplish God's plan. He ordains our steps. There is nothing coincidental in the life of a believer; all things work together to achieve the Father's will, and for the good of His people. Therefore, the people we connect with and make alliances with must have that same purpose in mind. We must be careful not to get "unequally yoked" with people who may take us on a different path, away from God's presence.

I feel impressed to highlight this. Many of us have liked to believe that we had the capacity, the ability, or enough love and will power to "change" people. We've convinced ourselves that they were waiting for us to get their life together and our light will be bright enough to illuminate their path. But the Lord is reminding us again that He is the one who knows all things and created all of humanity. Who are we to go where He did not send us? "You are not doing this for

---

[41] John 4:34

me, you're doing it to prove yourself a point. Is this worth losing your soul? Do you have so much time that you will be willing to waste it on the ones I did not send you to? I, the Lord search the heart of my people. I know them by their name. Before I formed them, I knew them" I hear the Lord saying, "My sheep know my voice, they listen."

Beloved, our God is calling us with such a power in His voice. It is a loud, thundering voice, the same sound a mother would make if her child was about to cross the street in front of a racing car or jump in front of a train. No! Stop! Don't do it! Whatever situation you find yourself in, I pray that you will hear God's voice and run back to Him. Maybe you got into the wrong relationship and you feel like you can't turn back, you already made a promise and now you feel stuck between a rock and a hard place, the Lord is saying "it's never too late to run back. Destroy the altars, I will open your eyes, and you will be able to see the things you could not see before. For a while, I was not, you could not hear me, you could not see me or feel my presence, but now you shall see what a great father you have. For your maker is your husband, the Lord of hosts, the One who keeps Israel."

11
RENEWING YOUR MIND

Rebuild. Renew. Reset. What will it take for you to trust again? Love again? Have you lost hope? Are you contemplating throwing in the towel? Can I say this? And you may already know it. It's not over until God says it is. You may not see any possible reconciliation, any change of behavior. You may have done everything in your power to make your marriage work. Every tentative of reconciliation have turned sour. You seem to have exhausted all your options. Great! Now, SIT. Submit. Invite. Trust. What if I told you nothing you did worked because you were the one doing it?
It may be time to let God guide you on this journey. Let Him show you the great things He has in store for you. it may look like something you've seen before. You may walk on familiar grounds, see familiar faces. You may need to go back to some dry and deserted land. You may experience some pain and discomfort, but can you trust the Lord? Can you trust that God is good and nothing will harm you? *"they will fight against you but will not overcome you, for I am with you and will rescue you," declares the LORD."* (Jeremiah 1:19)
I have not met one person who doesn't like the story of King David. He was a man after God's own heart. I believe most of us, if not all, would like to be considered men after God's own heart too. David was no saint, yet God favored him. David was not perfect, he simply trusted completely in the One who is perfect. He was meek, humble, and did not think too highly of himself.

He was unashamedly ignorant of a lot of things and found no issue turning to the Omniscient one.

Facing the past

Like David, we are ignorant of many things; we don't know it all, and that's perfectly fine. Before engaging in battle against his enemies, David would inquire of the Lord. Seeking God's direction and counsel was not a one-time thing with him – It was frequent. Even when the adversaries were known to him, even after he had already defeated them, David never relied on his previous victories, nor his failures. Please allow me to say this. Even when you think you've done everything you could, when you think you know the outcome of a situation, always seek the Lord. Be open to receive new instruction to face the same challenges, maybe using the same weapon. If God says it, He will do it. Your previous victories cannot guarantee future success, nor will your past failure determine an upcoming fiasco. That is why we cannot jump into familiar situations, using the same approach, same mindset. We must totally depend on our heavenly Father to call the shots.

Some situations can never get resolved unless you take a trip back in time. You must be willing to face the ghosts of the past, open some doors you thought were locked down. You may need to reopen some old wounds. Going back is not always negative. What if you ran so fast to get out that you left some valuable things behind? What if the key to your future is buried under the rubble of the past? Would you allow yesterday to rob you of tomorrow? Trust the Lord your God, He will certainly finish what He has started. He never leaves anything incomplete. Let Him take you back so that He can heal, cleanse, restore you. I recently went on a weekend prayer retreat with two amazing sisters in the Lord. The theme was "Let go and Let God". It was a weekend, I'm sure, none of us will forget. We had to face the demons of our past, address some serious, and even painful memories. We had to unlock doors we wish never existed. But let me tell you, it was worth it. I almost regretted not having done it sooner. When the Lord asked me to write my first book, *Let your pain speak*, I was very skeptical, reluctant. I didn't really understand what was so important about my life that He wanted me to share. So, when I had to open about the sexual abuse in my childhood, the sudden death of my beloved father, I honestly did not allow myself or the Lord to bring back the emotions, the pain, the real feeling I've experienced. It was too painful, too ugly. I felt too ashamed and embarrassed and wanted to move quickly onto something else. But that weekend with my two prayer warriors was a "do or die". There was no way I could carry this weight, anymore. My heavenly Father would not let me carry it – telling the truth, the weight didn't bother me at all, I could barely feel it; I had gotten so used to it. He wanted to set me free, completely. I am not asking you to wait until you go on a retreat, nor am I telling you the only way to heal is to write a book, but if that's what it takes, then do it — what I'm saying is trusting God and allowing His power to manifest in your life will set you free.

Allow me to share the words he then told me "let go of the past, let go of the lies of the enemy. I will take the hurt and the pain out of it and let you keep the memories". I now realize that when He said to "let my pain speak", it meant to share my testimony without ever feeling the pain, the guilt or the shame of it. We are not what had happened to us. We can choose to let God reveal our scars, our failures, our mistakes without ever feeling humiliated. He is our healer. He is our Maker. Let Him use the broken pieces of your past to build something wonderful. Don't let your relationship die because of what happened yesterday. Don't settle for the replica because you are too afraid to love and trust again.

Living as One

There may be a lot going on in your marriage at this hour. It might look more like a roommate type of situation. Everyone has their separate corner – doing their own things. The only thing you have in common may be the house, the kids or the dog. No communication, no plans together, no sex. Nothing. Again, if God is in it, He will make a way out of nothing. Where do you start? Prayer. Don't pray for your spouse. Pray for yourself. Invite the Holy Spirit to dwell in your heart. Take full control over your thoughts, your feelings, your actions, your words. Your marriage will never change unless you allow God to change YOU. Let Him take you back to the basics.

If communication is an issue, ask Him to change your heart. For out of the abundance of your heart, your mouth will speak[42]. He will anoint your lips to speak words that honor your spouse and reflect His glory. Be an encourager, not a naysayer. Uplift and support: you are your spouse's most important cheerleader. Watch out for the words you speak and even the unspoken words. Actions speak louder than words. If you haven't learned how to declare positive words over your life, how would you be able to speak like into your circumstances or over your spouse? How do I do that? I'm glad you asked. Spend time in the

---

[42] Luke 6:45

Word of God. That's the only place you will find the truth concerning you, your spouse, your marriage. Then, forgive yourself, your spouse and everyone else who hurt you – for you will be creating more space for the Holy Spirit to fill with His fruit (love, joy, peace, patience, kindness, goodness, gentleness, faithfulness, self-control). Finally, pray for your spouse and pray with your spouse. If praying together sound like speaking in a foreign language, ask the Master Teacher to teach you. God is not concerned about the words you say, He is pleased with your willingness to become a cord of three strands.

If trust and respect are the constant topics of discussion in your home, let God change your perspective. Let him teach you how to submit, how to trust, how to obey. Just ask. If any man lacks wisdom, let him ask of God (James 1:5). What does wisdom have to do with trust and respect? Everything. The wise woman builds her house, but the foolish destroys it with her own hands[43]. If a wife cannot trust and respect her husband, she will be destroying her own marriage. Therefore, wives must seek wisdom. Every time a wife is disrespectful to her husband, she disrespects the commandments of the Lord. Husbands are not exempt from trusting their wives, either for they watch over the affairs of their household...and their husband praise them. (proverbs 31) If you believe you are part of the same body, should you not trust each other? Take a look at your relationship. Is there any area you have not yet submitted to the Lord? Are you walking in unity in all aspects or do you keep some lanes closed with the yellow, "do not cross" tapes? It may be your children from a previous relationship, your

---

[43] Proverbs 14:1

family, your career goals, your finances, your challenges. How about your heart? Married people sometimes will share their bed, material possessions, everything else, but they will keep their hearts under lock. There will be spaces where they will not allow their spouse to enter. Some will refuse to share their painful childhood memories, family secrets or the like. If God cannot bless who you pretend to be, your spouse cannot love who you are not. We are meant to love and respect, defend and protect, provide and nurture each other.

Is sex and intimacy a struggle in your marriage? Have you bought into the lies of the enemy? Sex is a wonderful gift from God to married people. It is an expression of our innermost feelings, desires. It draws us closer to our spouse and allows us to join, not just our bodies, but our souls together. Whatever you've allowed to rob you of the joy of becoming one, on the most intimate level, it can be restored. God can restore your dignity, your connection, your intimacy with your spouse. Infidelity cannot and must not be the norm in your marriage. Our God is faithful. If we are called to be like Christ, we cannot claim unfaithfulness as a part of our DNA. For we are made new in Christ Jesus, our Lord. We are filled with the power of the Holy Spirit and bear the fruit of the Spirit. Faithfulness is the fruit, the evidence of the fullness of God in our life. We cannot call ourselves Christians, children of the Most High, sons and daughters of the King and accept to walk in darkness, in sin. Yes, we do not overcome by our own power, but by the grace of our God. Nevertheless, grace can never serve as an excuse to continue doing the same mistakes. For God grace is also the power given to us to resist temptation, the strength to overcome evil, to be transformed and renewed. It's more than the constant forgiveness of our sins. It goes beyond the unmerited favor of God. Let us not confuse God's mercy with His grace. Did he not tell Apostle Paul that, through the grace He's given him, Paul will be able to endure trials of all kinds? "My grace is sufficient for you' for my strength is made perfect in weakness[44]".

God hates divorce

"For I hate divorce!" says the LORD, the God of Israel[45]*."* We cannot even count the number of times this verse is used in a single day! God hates divorce. Of course, He does, He is the one who created marriage. Why would He want to see His design be ruined? Marriage is an absolute reflection of God's intent to commune with mankind. He is the husband, we are the bride. There is no separation between us – or so he desires. Did you know that God loves you more than He hates divorce? What do I mean? He will never vouch for you to put your life in peril because you wish to save something that He knows was long gone or never existed. We may be able to lie to ourselves, lie to others, but we can never lie to the One who know the number of hairs on our head. Too many people have tried to hide behind this verse to justify the worst marital situations, domestic violence, every form of abuse, lies and deceptions. I see women staying in marriage with a man they know is homosexual, but they're being asked to keep the appearances. Many live a double life, have more than one wife and many children, spending half of their time with one family and the other half with the other. How many have accepted the cheating, the lying, the sexual misconducts, the secrets as their fate? For they say, God hates divorce. Have you reduced marriage to having the same last name, dividing the

---

[44] 2 Corinthians 12:9
[45] Malachi 2:16 NLT

bills in half or living under the same roof? Is this God's view of marriage? Marriage is more than having a ring on the finger, a man in the house paying the bills, warming up your sheets. It's more than a woman in your bed, cooking, cleaning, taking care of your house. We cannot reduce marriage to sex or other pleasures of the flesh. Let us read, in its entirety, the scripture that we so conveniently like to use to justify our selfish choices.

"You cry out, "Why doesn't the LORD accept my worship?" I'll tell you why! Because the LORD witnessed the vows you and your wife made when you were young. But you have been unfaithful to her, though she remained your faithful partner, the wife of your marriage vows. **Didn't the LORD make you one with your wife? In body and spirit, you are his. And what does he want? Godly children from your union. So, guard your heart; remain loyal to the wife of your youth.** "For I hate divorce!" says the LORD, the God of Israel. "To divorce your wife is to overwhelm her with cruelty," says the LORD of Heaven's Armies. **"So, guard your heart; do not be unfaithful to your wife."** Malachi 2:14-16 NLT

I think I can rightly state that without unfaithfulness, the word "divorce" would have probably never been mentioned. Divorce is a byproduct of our unfaithfulness. That's what it leads us to. We cannot say God hates divorce and condone unfaithfulness. The vows we make to each other are sacred and that's why marriage must never be taken lightly. It's not a requirement to achieve our life purpose. Not everyone is called to marry but if and when we decide to join in covenant with another person, we must be clear about the Lord's expectations. Do you remember the dream I've had about abortion? How the Lord changed my perspective, so that today I can unequivocally say, I am pro-life, I stand against abortion and pray God's will to come? Why? Because when we seek God, and we ask Him to give us our heart desires, well, He does not just reveal to us the things He loves and the ones He hates, He causes our views to align with His. *"In your relationships with one another, have the same mindset as Christ Jesus"* (Philippians 2:5).

Don't stay in relationships that bring no glory to God. So, what should you do? Pray and ask Him to reveal you His plan, His will. Don't be afraid to seek His face. Be clear about the expectations He has laid out for you. For some, divorce might be the solution. Not because God has changed His mind about it, but because His will was never that you will be in this relationship, to begin with. Remember Judges 2 *"you shall not make a covenant with the people of this land, but you shall break down their altars.' Yet you have disobeyed me."*. There are some alliances God never meant for us to enter. You may think, "well I invested too much in this to quit. I have too much to lose". Is pleasing a man more important than pleasing God? How much more of God's treasure are you willing to waste? Do you want to keep on giving your pearls to swine?

For others, you must be willing to let go of what you have and let God build new. Let him give you a new perspective, change your mind, teach you what this was all about. Let him take you where you have not yet allowed him to carry you. Let the Lord rebuild! For if your marriage is built on the solid rock, no storm, no rain, no winds would ever take it apart. It's not over. God will restore everything that the enemy has stolen. He will make the dry bones come alive, if only you let Him change your thinking, reshape your perspective. Do not be conformed to the old patterns of your marriage, let the Holy Spirit transform your life.

12
RETURNING TO HIM

There are many uncertainties in life. If there's one thing we can be certain of, it's God's love for His people. His love is enough to make us whole again. Times and times again, we've witnessed God's people stray from the path He had set for them; they turned away and worshiped idols or other foreign gods. Yet, He never turned his back on them, always sending His prophets, one after the other to show the way back. Well, today is not different. He will use anyone and everyone to gather His lost sheep and bring them back home.

Whether you've experienced it before, God's love is real. He will stop at nothing to speak into the life of His loved ones. His love and mercy go beyond what our carnal minds can comprehend.

Throughout this book, I tried to highlight the various ways we destroy the sacred relationship we have with our God and with our spouse, not to bring condemnation or guilt, but with the hope to shed some light on the things that may be drawing us out of the Father's presence. You and I will never be able to fix the mess we put ourselves in, the chaos we created around us, and you want to hear the good news? He never expected us to – the only thing He's asking from us is to turn around and run back into His loving arms. Even if we had eternity, we will never be able to make things right, put our ducks in a row. It simply is humanly impossible. If we think it's our responsibility, we deny the powerful blood of Jesus

Christ that was shed on the cross to give us access to the one who loved us first. Only the love of the Father, the blood of the Son, the power of the Holy Spirit can make us stand in the presence of the Holy One. We can no longer live like sheep without shepherd and Jesus cannot be an afterthought in our life.

He is the beginning and the end. He loves you, as you are. But he needs you to come back to him with a repentant heart. It doesn't matter how many times you fell short, it doesn't matter how bad you messed up. God knew it before it even happened and He still hasn't changed his mind about you. His plans remain the same: to prosper you, to give you hope and a future (Jeremiah 29:11). But you won't know that unless you come closer. How can you trust what He says? "My people are being destroyed because they don't know me.[46]" . Our God is calling you into a higher level of intimacy. He doesn't want you to stand on the shoreline and shout; He needs for you to walk on the water and draw near. He wants to hear your heartbeat, just like he wants to let you hear His soft and tender whisper –the bride and her bridegroom. Did you ever think the relationship He had in mind was that of a master with His servant, a boss with his employee? He wouldn't have paid such a high price for you to remain so distant. No. Jesus calls you into his courts. He wants you to experience the fullness of his love, the joy of his presence.

> *"But then I will win her back once again.*
> *I will lead her into the desert*
> *and **speak tenderly to her there**.*
> *I will return her vineyards to her*
> *and transform the Valley of Trouble into a gateway of hope. She will give herself to me there,*

---

[46] Hosea 4:6 NLT

> *as she did long ago when she was young,*
> *when I freed her from her captivity in Egypt.*
> *When that day comes," says the LORD,*
> ***"you will call me 'my husband'***
> ***instead of 'my master'.*** [47] *"*

Can you see why He is calling your name and it's not to enslave you. It's not this long list of do's and don'ts that many people assume Christianity is about. It is a beautiful alliance, a sacred covenant, a wonderful relationship based on love and trust. Did it ever cross your mind that the reason why you feel like you are on a deserted land is to be closer to God? What if God knew this will be the only time He could have your undivided attention? But what happens when we find ourselves, alone, away from everyone or anything we are used to? We fuss and complain – find ways to run out as fast as we can. I'll tell you, the time to run is over. The time to make excuses are over. Time to shy away and crawl up because of guilt or fear is over. Of course, this may be new. You may not know what to do, or what to say. It may be very unfamiliar but God never called us to be familiar with Him. Doesn't familiarity lead to contempt? He wants you to feel comfortable in His presence, not familiar. You can never predict God's move. He will always surprise you, but He will never scare you. In His presence, you will always be safe.

Now He wants you to keep the vows you made to your spouse. He wants you to honor the promise you made to love and respect, to honor and cherish. It doesn't matter whether you are a seasoned preacher, Sunday school teacher, great evangelist... It really doesn't matter whether you can quote the entire bible from Genesis to Revelation or whether you serve every

---

[47] Hosea 2:14-16 NLT

Sunday in church. It doesn't matter if you can pray from dusk till dawn. All that matters is: can you obey the Lord's commands? Can you love your neighbor as you love yourself? Do you treat your spouse with kindness, love and decency? You may not cheat on your spouse, but if you don't treat them with respect, if you rebel against everything they say, if you do not protect your relationship, or do not fulfill the responsibilities of a husband or a wife, do not cater to their physical, emotional, spiritual or financial needs, it's all the same. Both men and women have pronounced the sacred vows of marriage on the day of their wedding. They will both be held accountable. Women are not the only ones who must live up to these standards.

"Hear the word of the LORD, O people of Israel! The LORD has brought charges against you, saying: "There is no faithfulness, no kindness, no knowledge of God in your land. You make vows and break them; you kill and steal and commit adultery. There is violence everywhere— one murder after another. That is why your land is in mourning, and everyone is wasting away." (Hosea 4:1-3 NLT).

Can you also hear him say: *"Return, faithless people; I will cure you of backsliding."*? And we shall reply: **"Yes, we will come to you, for you are the LORD our God."** (Jeremiah 3:22)

Father God, I thank you for the person who is reading these last lines. I ask that you forgive them for all their trespasses. And because I know what a wonderful and awesome God you are, I also trust that you will extend your mighty hand to rescue them, to draw them back to you. I ask that whatever situation they find themselves in, you will show your love once again, heal their hearts, renew their minds and transform their life, their marriage. I pray that you will give them wisdom to make the necessary adjustments, make the decisions that will bring glory to your name. I pray for the marriages in need of a complete makeover. I pray for those who have not yet begun this beautiful marriage adventure, that you will guide them and speak to them in such a way that they will recognize you through every step they make. I decree and declare that water shall be turned into wine, the joy of marriage shall be restored, in the mighty name of Jesus, our Lord and Savior. Amen.

Coming out Soon

Alter Ego
Strength from within

ABOUT THE AUTHOR

Finding strength in her Faith, Camille Babin has a tremendous ability as an Author, Speaker and Marriage Coach to inspire, motivate people to draw closer to God, unlock their potential and reignite the fire and the passion within. Her wisdom and spiritual guidance have helped many find peace of mind, regain hope and confidence, and experience major breakthroughs. She lives in Georgia with her husband and their three boys.

Find out more www.camillebabin.com

Facebook & Instagram: camillebabinauthor

UNFAITHFUL HEARTS

All Scripture quotations, unless otherwise indicated, are taken from the Holy Bible, New International Version®, NIV®. Copyright ©1973, 1978, 1984, 2011 by Biblica, Inc.™ Used by permission of Zondervan. All rights reserved worldwide.

Scripture quotations marked (NLT) are taken from the Holy Bible, New Living Translation, copyright ©1996, 2004, 2015 by Tyndale House Foundation. Used by permission of Tyndale House Publishers, Inc., Carol Stream, Illinois 60188. All rights reserved.

www.ingramcontent.com/pod-product-compliance
Lightning Source LLC
LaVergne TN
LVHW051130080426
835510LV00018B/2326